The
New
Oxford
World
History

Mexico in World History

William H. Beezley

OXFORD
UNIVERSITY PRESS

OXFORD
UNIVERSITY PRESS

Oxford University Press, Inc., publishes works that further
Oxford University's objective of excellence
in research, scholarship, and education.

Oxford   New York
Auckland   Cape Town   Dar es Salaam   Hong Kong   Karachi
Kuala Lumpur   Madrid   Melbourne   Mexico City   Nairobi
New Delhi   Shanghai   Taipei   Toronto

With offices in
Argentina   Austria   Brazil   Chile   Czech Republic   France   Greece
Guatemala   Hungary   Italy   Japan   Poland   Portugal   Singapore
South Korea   Switzerland   Thailand   Turkey   Ukraine   Vietnam

Copyright © 2011 by Oxford University Press

Published by Oxford University Press, Inc.
198 Madison Avenue, New York, New York 10016

www.oup.com

Oxford is a registered trademark of Oxford University Press

Library of Congress Cataloging-in-Publication Data
Beezley, William H.
Mexico in world history/ by William H. Beezley.
p. cm. — (New Oxford World History)
Includes bibliographical references and index.
ISBN 978-0-19-515381-1 (hardcover : alk. paper) —
ISBN 978-0-19-533790-7 (pbk. : alk. paper)
1. Mexico—History.   I. Title.
F1226.B44 2011
972—dc22   2011007315

1 3 5 7 9 8 6 4 2

Printed in the United States of America
on acid-free paper

Frontispiece: A woman makes tortillas from boiled and ground corn kernels, ca.
1880–97. *Library of Congress, LC-DIG-det-4a27119*

Como siempre, para Blue

Contents

Editors' Preface

This book is part of the New Oxford World History, an innovative series that offers readers an informed, lively, and up-to-date history of the world and its people that represents a significant change from the "old" world history. Only a few years ago, world history generally amounted to a history of the West—Europe and the United States—with small amounts of information from the rest of the world. Some versions of the "old" world history drew attention to every part of the world *except* Europe and the United States. Readers of that kind of world history could get the impression that somehow the rest of the world was made up of exotic people who had strange customs and spoke difficult languages. Still another kind of "old" world history presented the story of areas or peoples of the world by focusing primarily on the achievements of great civilizations. One learned of great buildings, influential world religions, and mighty rulers but little of ordinary people or more general economic and social patterns. Interactions among the world's peoples were often told from only one perspective.

This series tells world history differently. First, it is comprehensive, covering all countries and regions of the world and investigating the total human experience—even those of so-called peoples without histories living far from the great civilizations. "New" world historians thus share in common an interest in all of human history, even going back millions of years before there were written human records. A few "new" world histories even extend their focus to the entire universe, a "big history" perspective that dramatically shifts the beginning of the story back to the big bang. Some see the "new" global framework of world history today as viewing the world from the vantage point of the Moon, as one scholar put it. We agree. But we also want to take a close-up view, analyzing and reconstructing the significant experiences of all of humanity.

This is not to say that everything that has happened everywhere and in all time periods can be recovered or is worth knowing, but that there is much to be gained by considering both the separate and interrelated stories of different societies and cultures. Making these connections is still another crucial ingredient of the "new" world history. It emphasizes connectedness and interactions of all kinds—cultural, economic, political, religious, and social—involving peoples, places, and processes. It makes comparisons and finds similarities. Emphasizing both the comparisons and interactions is critical to developing a global framework that can deepen and broaden historical understanding, whether the focus is on a specific country or region or on the whole world.

The rise of the new world history as a discipline comes at an opportune time. The interest in world history in schools and among the general public is vast. We travel to one another's nations, converse and work with people around the world, and are changed by global events. War and peace affect populations worldwide as do economic conditions and the state of our environment, communications, and health and medicine. The New Oxford World History presents local histories in a global context and gives an overview of world events seen through the eyes of ordinary people. This combination of the local and the global further defines the new world history. Understanding the workings of global and local conditions in the past gives us tools for examining our own world and for envisioning the interconnected future that is in the making.

Bonnie G. Smith
Anand Yang

Preface

In 2010, Mexico celebrated both the bicentennial of its independence and the centennial of its revolution. These two events shaped Mexican nationality and refined its twin legacies of a significant pre-Columbian indigenous heritage and, in terms of language and religion, a foundational colonial experience. These celebrations drew positive attention to the nation, which has recently been known largely for the violence associated with the illegal drug trade. Observers recalled Mexico's international presence based on its primary role in the early days of the United Nations and as the host of the 1968 Olympic Games and the 1970 and 1986 World Cup competitions. Moreover, Mexico has popular recognition around the globe for its distinctive cuisine, its television and movie stars, and its unmistakable music.

Tacos and tequila have worldwide popularity. Taco stands can be found in the Alaskan Arctic, Saudi Arabia, Japan, Thailand, Australia, across South America, in Cape Town, and nearly everywhere in between. Tequila, once associated only with Mexican *borrachos* (drunkards) has become, like martinis or scotch, another international drink. Mexican *telenovelas* (soap operas) have earned global recognition, and several have become national sensations in Japan and Russia, while the movies have made celebrities of such characters as the professional wrestler El Santo and the avenging horseman El Charro Negro—one Colombian guerrilla leader in the 1950s adopted "El Charro Negro" as his revolutionary name in memory of his youthful days watching Mexican movies. Mariachi music, with the musicians in typical sombreros, bolero jackets, and tight pants (or skirt in the case of women mariachis) have inspired imitators in Japan, prompted mariachi bar mitzvahs in Los Angeles, California, and resulted in about a half dozen pages of telephone listings for bands in Bogotá, Colombia. The international reputation of Mexico rests of course with tourists, most of whom know the beaches, especially those on the Gulf coast associated with magnificent Maya ruins.

The global concern about the Americanization of world culture has ignored the fact that today Mexico's great influence is felt widely in the nearby United States: from the ubiquitous tacos and quesadillas of fast-food drive-throughs to enchiladas and mole of upscale restaurants

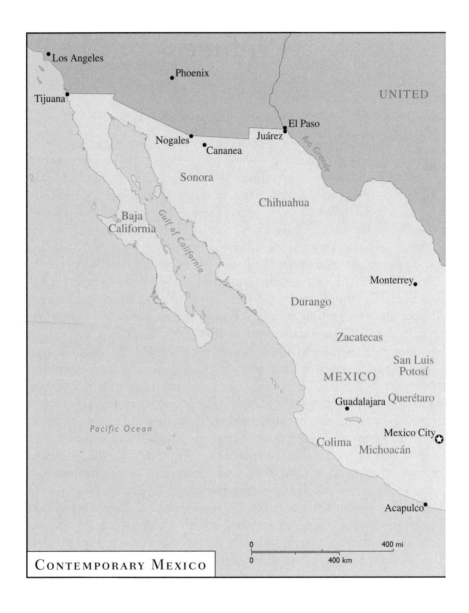

CONTEMPORARY MEXICO

to the tortillas, refried beans and other ingredients at grocery stores. Salsa has exceeded ketchup as a condiment for more than a decade, and chips and salsa have become a common appetizer in homes and cafés. Spanish is heard everywhere from businesses that offer help *en Español* to television and radio broadcasts to popular music and movies. A Mexican-owned soccer team, Chivas USA, plays in the United States professional league, and Mexican golfers, such as Lorena Ochoa, the

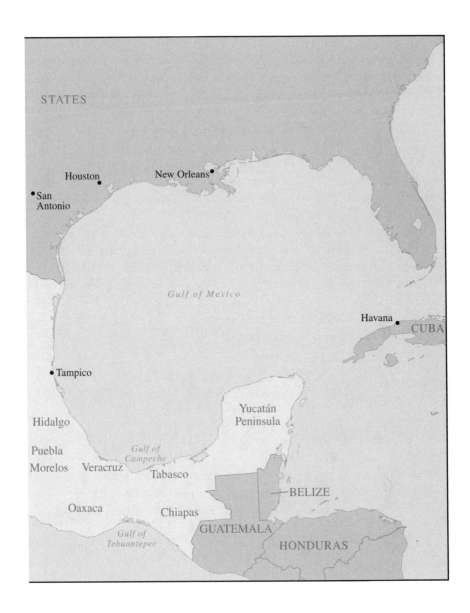

top woman in the world until her retirement, and other athletes have succeeded in the U.S. professional leagues.

The Mexican national soccer team, called the Tri for the tricolor flag, regularly plays matches in the United States. The major holiday of Cinco de Mayo, often mistaken as Mexican Independence Day, has community sponsorship and brewery patronage across the United States, especially in the Southwest. At the same time, Mexican soft drinks, especially Coca-

Cola made with natural cane sugar, and alcoholic beverages, including Corona beer, aged tequila, and the margarita cocktail, have claimed passionate followers. Fashion items ranging from ponchos to shawls to guayaberas, the popular Yucatán shirts, provide a balance to tank tops, tourist T-shirts and hooded sweatshirts advertising one or another Cancún bar.

Yet for all its presence across the globe that makes Mexico seem familiar, there is little general knowledge about the nation and its people's history and culture. This book provides a concise introduction that should offer guidance to broader themes in the historical legacies, fascinating heritage, and unexpected diversity of cultures and ethnicities that constitute the Mexican experience.

The great pre-Columbian civilizations have long enthralled the general public as well as museum directors and university professors. A sense of wonder appears in questions about the Maya writing system, Aztec hydroengineering, and Meso-American calendars that had remarkable accuracy. The domestication of corn and then its elaboration into multiple forms of soups, drinks, and various tortillas seem to match the apparent artistic sensibilities evident in the architecture and stone carving. The practical innovations and artistic capabilities clash with religious practices that demanded self-mutilation and human sacrifice. Yet the excavated and restored monuments with their pyramids and ball courts continue to haunt the imagination.

Anticolonial and anti-imperial beliefs notwithstanding, during its 300-year existence the colony of New Spain had an enduring impact. Today Mexican life remains infused with the Spanish language (although certainly recognizable as Mexican Spanish), Roman Catholicism (again with a Mexican character), and Mediterranean popular practices, including leisure activities, suffused the everyday culture. This is Spain's legacy to its largest, richest, and most diverse colony.

Independence in 1821 changed the political system, commercial relationships, and little else. Certainly during the first half of the nineteenth century, leaders tried to make social and cultural changes (restricting the activities of the church outside of religious matters, for example); these efforts not only failed but resulted in political instability and foreign indebtedness. Many observers credit these debts for foreign invasions that, in case of the U. S.–Mexican War resulted in the loss of half of the national territory. Nevertheless, the nation endured. In the last quarter of the century it witnessed modernization along the path of other industrial nations, relying on foreign investors to finance both railroads and textile factories as the country continued to export both silver and agricultural products. The uneven distribution of the benefits and profits of this development program ultimately resulted in the popular uprising, the 1910 revolution.

The men and women who took up arms to remake their nation did so against huge odds. Quickly they exceeded their political goals and fought for a new nation offering equality in politics, justice, labor, and among social groups, especially the indigenous and women. This endeavor demanded land reform, labor organization, widespread education, and government restrictions on the two major threats to these programs, the Catholic Church and foreign investors. This popular uprising, before the Russian, the Chinese, or the Cuban upheavals, was the world's first social revolution.

The Mexican Revolution deserves recognition both for its accomplishments and for what the various leaders attempted. It has become popular for historians to attempt to write without dwelling on the actions of great, especially male, leaders to avoid what is called both "top-down" and "patriarchal" histories. This is sometimes a mistake, and certainly it is in regard to the revolution. The popular leaders, a list that must include Francisco Madero, Venustiano Carranza, Alvaro Obregón, Plutarco Calles, and in particular Pancho Villa and Emiliano Zapata, should be recognized, because during their revolutionary careers they enlarged the goals, dreams, hopes, and sense of the possible for others. The psychologist Carl Jung dubbed this kind of identification between leaders and followers "psychic inflation," and this is exactly what the revolutionary generals provided to their troops and supporters. Call it psychic inflation, pride, or self-worth—these revolutionary chiefs inspired it. This growth of pride helps explain how the national or regional leaders recruited men and women in the far-flung remote communities.

At the very least, the revolutionary generals and presidents created a sense of new national possibilities for a generation. Then their sons and daughters came to power. The new generation shifted interest to middle-class programs that were so extensive they allowed, if they did not encourage, corruption. During the second half of the twentieth century, the revolution remained—at least in political language, popular imagination, and the folklore of movies; but the political expressions were hollow—only the fervid rhetoric of official institutions. A series of shocks, almost on a once-a-decade schedule, wracked the nation and its people: the 1968 Student Massacre, the 1970s peso devaluations, the 1985 earthquake, and the 1994 EZLN (Zapatista National Liberation Army) revolt against the North American Free Trade Agreement and constitutional reforms ending the communal land institution as well as the legacy of neglect for indigenous peoples. These events and others such as the rise in ethnic politics, illegal migration to the United States, and the advent of an illegal drug culture eroded what remained of the revolution as the expression of the nation and its people, and ultimately concluded in the 2000 election of President Vicente Fox, who defeated the official revolutionary party as the first victorious opposition candidate.

Tracing the political pattern in sweeping strokes ignores the dramatic creation of the nation's culture, or better said, its cultures. From the earliest settlements through the colonial experience and the independent history, diversity has remained paramount in Mexico. The multitude of landscapes, natural life, and human cultures exceed those of nearly everywhere else in the world. There is not one kind of corn or maize, but more than half a dozen, and this staff of daily life reflects the overall variety that characterizes national life as it appears in music, for example, or religious devotions or textile weavings. Saying that Mexican cultural life is a tapestry of many threads, while a cliché, has vibrancy because of its veracity.

This brief sketch only hints at some of the most dramatic moments of Mexico's past, but it does offer the historical framework that provides the context for the pressing issues of illegal drug-related violence, hysterical political responses to illegal immigrants in Arizona, and the efforts of the Mexican and U.S. governments to balance migration and jobs. The narrative allows a glimpse of the passion, endurance, and trials of the people. These are individuals who have created first a culture and then a nation that not only aspires to diversity but also expresses it through the multiplicity of ethnicities, cultures, and landscapes that together are Mexico.

Mexico in
World History

First Cultures and Indigenous Empires

According to the Maya, even the gods are not perfect, and they are not always that easy to please. Tepeu and Gucumatz, whom the Maya called the creators, directed the god Huracán to make the earth and it inhabitants. His first efforts failed as he made men and women of mud, who dissolved, and then of wood, who lacked hearts. So Huracán destroyed these attempts with a tremendous rainstorm and flood. He tried again and found success when he formed a dough made from maize, a kind of corn, to create the Maya. The Maya priests used hieroglyphs to compose their sacred book, the Popol Vuh,[1] where they recorded their origins as the people of maize.

Years later, the Aztecs, too, told of their creation. In their myth, the god Ometeotl gave birth to four Tezcatlipoca, gods who represented the cardinal directions, major colors, geographic features, and moral qualities. In the east, the White Tezcatlipoca, Quetzalcoatl, presided over light, mercy, and wind; in the south, the Blue Tezcatlipoca, Huitzilopochtli, ruled over war; in the west, the Red Tezcatlipoca, Xipe Totec, dominated gold, farming, and springtime; and in the north, the Black Tezcatlipoca, known only by this name, exercised authority over judgment, night, deceit, sorcery, and the earth. Four times these gods in turn attempted to create a world associated with a sun, but each one ended in destruction—by jaguars, wind, fire, and finally water—because the gods became unhappy with the people or with each other's efforts.

Quetzalcoatl decided to re-create the people after the fourth destruction and went to the underworld, where he stole their bones and dipped them in his own blood to resurrect them. They formed the Aztecs, the people of the fifth sun, governed by Huitzilopochtli, their world destined to end in earthquakes. Their survival depended on the daily struggles that matched Huitzilopochtli against the moon and stars. His strength came from the hearts and blood of mankind, and his weapons were made of obsidian, the volcanic glass common to Mexico's volcanoes. In an effort to aid Huitzilopochtli, the Aztecs went to war to capture victims for sacrifice, using weapons and sacrificial knives also made of obsidian. In thin pieces, obsidian holds a sharpness that makes it ideal as a point for spears or arrows and as a blade for swords and knives. Today it is used as a scalpel blade. The Aztecs also polished it to function as a mirror. They prized its rich colors of green to black and its reflective character that gave it a desirable quality in decoration. Above all, it allowed them to aid in Huitzilopochtli's struggles to preserve the world.[2]

These origin myths tell of gods at play with maize dough or in struggles using obsidian knives that created the men and women of Mexico's pre-Columbian cultures. Little in the way of evidence supports the divine books, but there can be no doubt that maize became the primary foodstuff in the region, and, for peoples without bronze, tin, or iron, obsidian, much more than flint, provided the material for tools, weapons, and even jewelry. In this way, corn and obsidian created these ancient societies. But looking even further back in the archaeological record, scholars find another driving force: migration.

On a clear night, the sky above what today we call Mexico becomes luminous with stars. This sky, in its solitude, promises adventure and opportunity to those who take risks. Prehistoric Asian men and women saw the night sky, and some dared to seek its limits. They roamed to the east, the origin of the night, the stars, and the sun that followed, and eventually crossed a land bridge, called Beringia, between Asia and North America that today has disappeared below the waves, except for its vestiges, the Aleutian Islands. The passage existed because of the lower level of the Pacific Ocean. These wanderers arrived in North America around 40,000 years ago and continued to come in successive waves for several thousand years. Other small groups arrived in the Americas by sea, on the west coast from both Asia and the South Sea Islands, and on the east coast, perhaps from Africa, across the Atlantic. These travelers became the indigenous residents of the Americas, whose descendants included the Maya and the Aztecs. At least this is their origins as pieced together by archaeologists, geologists, and anthropologists.

One conceit of the modern world holds that today people have the distinction of mobility, traveling often between nations and continents for new lives, employment, business, and pleasure. For the residents of Mexico, this is not a recent development; they have traveled throughout their history. Based on the first evidence of men and women, identified by archaeologists working in excavations from central Mexico north into Alaska and the Aleutian Islands, they were travelers, who sought new, more hospitable, and less dangerous locations in which to live. Archaeological excavations of campsites and grave sites and a few cave etchings tell little else about motives and daily life beyond their hunting and gathering for food.

The land they discovered seemed endless, with great biological diversity that ranks fifth today among the world's countries for number of species—more than 1,000 species of birds, 640 reptiles, 450 mammals, 330 amphibians, and insects too numerous to count. These species live in diverse habitats that offered the earliest peoples opportunities to live well, but with the staggering diversity came challenges as well. The entire area is periodically threatened by deadly droughts, hurricanes, and earthquakes. Each of these found personification in the Popol Vuh and other indigenous records, as a god in the region's early cultures. The need for rain resulted in the widespread devotion to Chac (Maya) or Tlaloc (Aztec), the god of rain; disruption and death from tropical rainstorms became the god Huracán, from which English speakers derive the word *hurricane*. Early peoples also revered Kisin, god of the underworld and earthquakes, and Tonatiuh, who was expected to bring the world to an end.

Until about 8000 BCE, the nomadic peoples lived on grasses and nuts, generally collected by women. Men often hunted mammoths and other large animals but with little success, based on animal skeletal evidence. The development of stone spear points and the spear throwing device called the atlatl, which improved their hunting success, did not change the reliance on gathered foods. Even those peoples on the coast and along rivers who had occasional access to fish lived chiefly on plant foods. Sometime around 2000 BCE, these nomads made critical changes as they developed the beginning of both agriculture and village life.[3]

By accident or invention, early people developed small-patch agriculture and settled into more permanent villages. These two new food and living patterns in some ways have continued until the present. It is likely that women, who gathered the seeds and grasses eaten by their families, first noticed the connections between seeds, growing plants, and edible crops.[4] This critical discovery eventually led to the domestication of maize, or native corn, which was used in the staple food item, the tortilla. The advent of agriculture occurred in the Balsas River basin in southern Mexico around 3600 BCE and was soon followed by the domestication of a complex of plants that quickly became the basic foodstuffs of Mexico. Beyond corn, the new diet included beans, which provided a rich source of protein, and chilies, which supplied vitamin C, aided digestion, and acted to cool individuals through the evaporation of sweat. To this trio of foods, these prehistoric villagers soon added squash, a source of carbohydrates and liquids, especially important in arid places.

For easier digestion, women boiled corn before grinding and beans before mashing. In regions with limited firewood for fuel, generally small fires sufficed, especially for the making of tortillas that served as edible wraps for the beans and other foods. When cooked hard, the tortillas could be preserved for long periods. Historians know of the significance of tortillas from their frequent portrayal in hieroglyphs and engravings and on pottery. Garden patches and small villages allowed some time for other occupations such as making of rudimentary pottery and weaving of cloth from wild cotton. More settled life allowed some men and women to become full-time religious leaders who focused on pleasing gods helpful to the community, especially the corn god and the rain god.

Gods and men bargained, exchanging good crops and new techniques for offerings of precious possessions—at least that is how later peoples explained developments during what is now called the Formative Era, 2000 BCE to 200 CE. Anthropologists suggest that trial-and-error experiences led to agricultural innovations. The people had other answers. How else to explain developments in agriculture that included irrigation and terracing except as gifts from a benign god? How else to explain blood offerings through self-inflicted wounds, small animals, and selected victims except to offer thanks to the gods? Improved harvests enabled the population to grow and stratify. Because part of the population had extra time beyond seeking subsistence, they began to invest in elaborate architecture. Their grander ceremonial centers soon included stone columns that provided carved records of the genealogy of community leaders.

For centuries, these peoples remain nameless, known only through excavation of scattered settlements. Not until the emergence of the Olmec culture, around 1600 BCE, do the shrouds of mystery part. The Olmec culture epitomized civilization based on maize agriculture and social diversification. The Olmecs made blood offerings, perhaps as bargains with their gods, associated with the stars and the sun, their crops and rain. Though the Olmecs stand out during this era, other peoples in the region adopted similar patterns in social and economic life.

The Olmecs refined their culture in the ceremonial centers of San Lorenzo and La Venta, in the tropic zone of the modern Mexican states of Veracruz and Oaxaca. At these sites, the Olmecs invented new constructions that today characterize Formative Era life. They built elaborate temples, ball courts, and marketplaces. They used mounds of earth as the base for pyramid-shaped temples that reached above the trees, with a chapel containing an altar on top of each. Priests, archaeologists have determined, climbed the pyramids and observed the stars, monitored the transit of the sun, and made offerings to the gods.

Each of these centers, and other urban locations, had ball courts. These structures, built in ravines or dug-out sites, had the shape of a barbell. At each end, they posted a kind of basketball hoop, turned vertically. Based on hieroglyphs and wall paintings archaeologists believe that the players competed in a contest with a hard rubber ball, trying to put the ball through the hoop using only their feet, legs, chest, or head, never their hands. The contest (it is difficult to think of it as a game) provided a ceremony that predicted the future or determined community decisions (with each team representing one course of action or another) and demonstrated fate or honored the gods. Once an individual scored, the ceremony ended, and at least on occasion the priests sacrificed one player on the top of a pyramid. Whom did the priests offer to the gods— winner or loser? The evidence in carved and pottery images remains inconclusive, but perhaps the Olmecs believed that the winner, through sacrifice, could come to join the gods.

The Olmecs may have commemorated these sacrificed heroes of the ball court in the massive heads that they carved. No other explanation exists for these colossal heads, the first of which was discovered in 1862, and the second not until 1942. The carvings reached over nine feet in height and forty tons in weight. Their passive faces seem to have Asian features, and their heads are always covered with some sort of helmet. These monumental carvings have been found only near the Olmec ceremonial centers. The Mexican government transported two to the national anthropology museum in the capital city, one of which stands at the entrance. The other fifteen known enormous carvings are in community museums, near where they were found, or in the Jalapa, Veracruz, Museum of Anthropology. The Olmecs also carved stone images of small, chubby figures, perhaps babies or eunuchs, often found in fields—suggesting that they served as offerings for crops or to attract rain. Certainly the carvings represented an effort by the Olmecs to connect to their gods.

Their ceremonial sites included plazas paved with limestone. Here they held markets for the exchange of agricultural products and other items, such as salt. A regular cycle of trading days soon followed. Indeed, these people had a preoccupation with the seasons, essential for agriculture and recording their momentous events. They devised a calendar system for planting crops and another for rituals, along with a method of record keeping. The agricultural calendar system combined eighteen months of 20 days each for a year of 360 days that ended with

This giant stone head (nine feet in height and weighing forty tons) from the ceremonial center of La Venta displays the lapidary skills of the Olmec culture on a massive scale. The purpose of the carvings remains mysterious, and their facial structures have inspired speculation about Asian origins of the Olmecs.
Werner Forman/ Art Resource, NY

a 5-day period that kept the calendar adjusted to the movement of the stars, sun, and seasons. The ritual calendar used 20 day symbols with thirteen numbers for a total ceremonial year that equaled 260 days. The two calendars coincided every fifty-two years, encompassing all of the month and day signs for a complete cycle, somewhat like today's century. These calendars were chiseled into stone. Individuals took their names from their date of birth, such as Four-Deer, suggesting an astrological belief in birth, name, and destiny tied to animals or plants as guardian spirits This practice allowed the Olmecs to record genealogies of their rulers in stone, identifying leaders and reigns with dates and glyphs that served as a kind of writing system.

The Olmec culture ended about 200 BCE. Scholars have offered several explanations for the Olmecs' disappearance, ranging from ecological changes to epidemic diseases to disastrous warfare.[5] The peoples who followed the Olmecs had weapons with points or blades that they fashioned from obsidian. These weapons aided the rise of the Maya and other peoples at the ceremonial centers of Teotihuacan and Monte Alban. The volcanic glass enabled the Maya and others to make more effective agricultural tools and weapons such as swords and spears. Those who had obsidian quickly embarked on wars of conquest and practiced more intense agriculture with the improved tools.

The Classic Era, from 200 BCE to 900 CE, refers to the time when Maya peoples lived primarily in the northeastern region of modern Guatemala known as the Petén. There they built a major ceremonial site at Tikal and another in Copán (in modern Honduras). They built four-side pyramids that towered above the rain forest trees, complexes of one-room apartment-like dwellings for the residents presumed to be priests and their families, market plazas, and ball courts. Yet these represent only material remnants of a society of which little else is known.

Paintings, carvings, and burial sites reveal a culture that believed some individuals could turn themselves into jaguars who prowled the night. Carvings of these creatures appeared in the ceremonial centers, while images of the rain god also predominate. These images suggest the Maya lived in a world filled with dangers and guardians, both of which required placation. They practiced constant personal and community rituals to maintain a balance with the spirit world.

The majority of the Maya peoples, the commoners, lived in dispersed agricultural communities outside the ceremonial centers. They practiced slash-and-burn agriculture, in which ashes served to fertilize the thin soil that could be farmed for three to five years, before the field had to be left fallow to recover. The system yielded larger harvests than the unfertilized plantings of earlier times. The increased food production allowed for greater diversification and specialization within the community. Merchants traveled to the coast to trade for salt, to the north (central Mexico) for obsidian, and to the south for precious objects, like iridescent Quetzal feathers. Artisans carved the stone columns with genealogies and histories. Ruler-priests, according to the Popol Vuh, communicated with the gods and directed the people through the cycle producing maize, beans, squash, and chilies. Quetzal feathers and jaguar skins served as ritual clothing for priests. Only the rulers lived in the ceremonial centers, supported by servants, artisans, and merchants, and focused on the performance of rituals and the study of the natural world.

Maya priests developed a remarkable calendar, more accurate than the ones in use elsewhere in the world, including Europe. Their mathematics used a base of 20, an unusual system. They devised the concept of zero, apparent in their numerical system, before Hindu mathematicians developed it and before it became part of the Arabic mathematics that eventually reached Europe. With mathematics and astronomy, they formulated a more sophisticated knowledge of their world. Their system of hieroglyphs—carved images of Mayas with elaborate headdresses, stone ear and lip plugs, and holdings feathers and weapons to identify their authority, with attached date symbols—enabled them to record the political and military achievements of their leaders in stone monuments.[6]

The Maya swept across the low country of Guatemala's Petén and into the bordering region of Mexico's Yucatán and Belize. They built centers similar in structure if not in size to Tikal. These Classic Era sites shared the characteristic structures of pyramids topped with a temple, sunken ball courts, and numerous columns, called *stelae*, covered with genealogical and historical information. These religious centers traded with one another, but they lacked political unity, and, as recorded on the stelae, they often fought among themselves.

What made these people Maya was a common language and shared beliefs. Their glyphs show aspects of their daily lives—the clothing, adornment, and activities, at least of the men and women who led their society. A sense of vanity appears in some customary practices, at least among these members of the upper ranks of society. Using a piece of wood strapped cross the forehead, they deformed the heads of babies or young children to create a distinctive sloping skull that extended the line of the nose. Extensive tattoos covered much of the body of priests and leaders, at least as we see them in the carved images and hieroglyphs on pyramid walls, in the remarkable murals painted on the walls of grave sites within the pyramids, and on the sophisticated ceramics made and decorated by Maya artisans. Stone adornments such as ear and lip plugs served as accessories to the woven cloth, jaguar skin, and rare-feather costumes. The individual completed his or her ensemble with long hair, often held in place by honey, styled to continue the slope of nose and forehead. The geometric lines and bright colors of Maya bodies and adornment display their pleasure in the aesthetics of precision that reflected their mathematical expertise.

Maya polytheistic religion involved powerful gods, especially Chac, who was responsible for rain. The Mayas favored their gods with blood offerings, either from self-mutilation or with the sacrifice of individuals—young women or prisoners taken in the incessant wars with neighboring Maya. Despite the common language, religion, and agriculture of this richly varied culture, the Maya remained divided. Yet their language, agriculture, religion built on maize, pyramids and ball courts, and calendar system became an enduring heritage to the peoples of Mexico.

Other societies existed in Mexico and upper Central America (called by anthropologists Meso-America). Two exemplary contemporary cultures, both known for their large ceremonial centers with the dramatic architecture of monumental pyramids and extensive market centers, were the people of Monte Alban, just outside the modern-day Oaxaca City, and of Teotihuacan, just north of Mexico City. Monte Alban belonged to the Zapotecs. From this ceremonial center, they dominated surrounding peoples, who lived in a series of subject cities. Monte Alban's hilltop had defensive advantages, but priests and leaders who lived there had to be supplied with water. Archaeologists who have excavated the site have found gold rings, bracelets, necklaces, and brooches that identify a culture of wealth beyond the customary use of obsidian. For funerary rites, the Zapotecs dressed dead priests in woven cloth of cotton and rare feathers, adorned with precious jewelry, and placed them in unmarked sites at Monte Alban. After some period, priests excavated the grave and painted the skulls and other bones a vibrant red. Despite their linguistic, artistic, and religious differences, the Zapotecs, like the other peoples of southern Mexico, shared the architecture of temples, the calendar of signs and numbers, and the use of corn and obsidian with the Maya. Excavation continues today, and the deciphering of the glyphs and murals has just begun at this and nearby sites that may reveal other major cities.

Even more haunting than Monte Alban are the size, beauty, and mystery of Teotihuacan, located in the valley of Mexico. The largest of these great centers of the Classic Era, it centered on the Pyramid of the Sun that rises more than 200 feet above the ground, today overlooking the ruins of a magnificent commercial center of more than twelve square miles. A ceremonial sector included a temple dedicated to Quetzalcoatl, the feathered serpent, and another one for the pantheon of the sun, moon, and rain gods. The prevailing explanation for the significance and wealth of Teotihuacan is that its people held a monopoly on obsidian, the volcanic glass essential for weapons, tools, decorations, and religious rituals obtained from the nearby volcanoes that today are called Popocatepetl and Iztaccihutal.

Teotihuacan, Monte Alban, and the classic Maya cities were abandoned by 800 CE. Scholars have not satisfactorily explained this. One possibility is that slash-and-burn agriculture eventually moved the farmers more than a day's journey from the ceremonial centers, creating problems for their participation in numerous rituals. Another explanation suggests that environmental disasters such as earthquakes or hurricanes destroyed the communities of the common people who supported the priests. Or, perhaps epidemics of pneumonia ravaged the populations. Another hypothesis proposes that outsiders conquered the region and ended the era.[7]

The Pyramid of the Sun was a religious site in the middle of Teotihuacan, the ceremonial and commercial center from 200 BCE to 900 CE. This pre-Aztec culture built a series of striking pyramids (the steps to the Pyramid of the Moon are also visible) used for blood sacrifices. Shutterstock

Scholars call the years after the collapse of these major centers the Post-Classic Era, covering the period from 800 CE until the arrival of the Spaniards in 1519. The Post-Classic peoples to a great extent built on the agricultural, architectural, artistic, scientific, recording, and calendric traditions of the eerie, abandoned ceremonial sites of earlier times. The rather hazy descriptions of previous cultures based almost exclusively on material objects gives way during the Post-Classic Era to pictographic records that reveal individuals and that provide personality to these civilizations. These later peoples seemed to have acquired many of the gods of their predecessors, such as Quetzacoatl, the rain god (called variously Tlaloc, Chac, and other names), and the sun god. This Post-Classic Era was a time of movement of whole communities, commercial travel, and military expansion, made possible with new technology of the bow and arrow and padded cotton armor.

In central Mexico, the people known as the Toltecs emerged. This civilization provided one of the fundamental narratives that bridged the indigenous era and the Spanish conquest. These peoples arrived in the region of central Mexico, according to their bark-paper books called codices. They likely migrated south from Zacatecas or even farther north, under their ruthless and efficient leader Mixcoatl (called by one historian a "Mexican Ghengis Khan").[8] They defeated local residents and established a center near Teotihuacan. At this point, the energetic, imaginative Mixcoatl was murdered by his brother, who had plans for further conquests in the region. The assassinated victim's wife escaped but then died bearing their heir, named for his birth date Ce Acatl Topiltzin. His name translates "One-Reed," likely 947 CE on the European calendar.

Ce Acatl became devoted to Quetzalcoatl. As the high priest in the service of this god, he adopted the god's name. He challenged his uncle to single combat to the death and defeated him. Quetzalcoatl then became the ruler of the Toltecs. He relocated their principal center to the northeast, where they built their ceremonial and political center. Called Tula, it earned an enduring reputation as an indigenous Shangri-la for music and literature cultivated under the gentle, innovative leadership of the human Quetzalcoatl. (Later the Aztecs destroyed Toltec codices and other records, so no examples survive.)

Quetzalcoatl soon reestablished the obsidian monopoly that had collapsed with the fall of Teotihuacan. With this wealth, Toltec society grew in size and accomplishments. In agriculture, the Toltecs developed terracing and irrigation for the first time in central Mexico. Their artistic practices in murals, pottery, feather painting, weaving, poetry, and singing extended beyond all earlier developments, but the humane ruler stumbled, according to legend, when he was introduced to pulque, the alcoholic beverage brewed from agave sap. After a night of tippling, he awoke to find himself in bed with his sister. In violation of the regulations of sobriety and also those against incest, he had to depart Tula. He left with a group of his closest associates to find redemption elsewhere. In every retelling of the departure, the legends and the histories recount the bearded, light-skinned Quetzalcoatl's promise to return, identifying a declaration fraught with portents.[9] This legend likely represented internal political struggles between Toltec rivals, perhaps over ritual offerings of jade, butterflies, and snakes, rather than human blood and hearts.[10] At any rate, the departure has been commemorated by Mexicans ever since, including the mural on the iconic library of the National Autonomous University of Mexico that features a stone boat marked with the feathery servant who carried him away.

Perhaps this legendary departure, repeated in Aztec codices, signified the initiation of a Toltec invasion of Yucatán, although Toltec influence may have reached the region through trade, not conquest. Once they arrived in the Yucatán Peninsula the Toltec warriors, traders, or both found that the center of revived Maya cultures, once located at Tikal, had shifted north. New ceremonial centers, where priests lived, were surrounded by small communities whose residents continued the slash-and-burn production of corn, beans, and chilies. The flourishing ceremonial centers at Uxmal, Chichen Itza, and Mayapan maintained a political and commercial alliance, called the League of Mayapan, for about two and half centuries (900 to 1150 CE), until they become divided over commercial profits and broke into warring factions. The league collapsed, and for the remainder of the Post-Classic Era the Maya peoples lived a decentralized, embattled existence marked by persistent warfare against each other and outsiders, punctuated by trade.

The Toltecs brought a definable influence to the Post-Classic Maya. The incorporation of the mythic feathery servant into the Maya pantheon (as KulKulcán), the appearance of the Chacmool sculptures of reclining male figures thought to be rain gods, and increased human sacrifice illustrate their influence on the Maya. These changes may have resulted from the invasion and occupation of the region by Toltecs or from close commercial ties between the two cultures. The towering pyramids, elaborate market centers, and many ball courts provide lasting monuments to Maya culture throughout the peninsula, even today.

The decline of the civilization centered at Monte Alban had been followed by the rise of other Mixtec and Zapotec peoples in the south during the Post-Classic Era. The Zapotecs established new ceremonial and ruling centers at Zaachila (near the base of the hilltop Monte Alban site) and Mitla, about fifty miles away. The beauty of the jewelry made of gold, jade, and other precious stones found in the burials at both sites suggest a wealthy, flourishing civilization adept at mineral working. In the highlands to the north and west, the Mixtec peoples established numerous communities. Various indications suggest a connection between the Toltecs and the Mixtecs, especially their aggressive nature, augmented by bows and obsidian-tipped arrows, the most deadly technology of the time. The Mixtecs came down from the highlands and successfully conquered the Zapotec centers, only to be forced out time and again. Different in language and background, the Mixtecs were highland peoples and the Zapotecs were lowlanders, reaching into tropic zones. They both farmed maize but used different species of the plant, and the highlanders employed techniques such as terracing that the lowlanders did not need in their flat environment.

The Mixtecs produced a large number of surviving books. These codices were actually fanlike folded sheets of deerskin and bark paper with glyphic accounts in brilliant colors. These beautiful narratives recorded the history, glories, gods, and life of the Mixtec and their leaders. Only now are scholars beginning to understand the depth and complexity of the information in the codices for such centers as Tlaxiaco and Teposcolula. Some fragments survive for each center, but others record events for all the Mixtec people. The Bodley and Selden Codices, both in the Bodleian Library at Oxford, contain information on the Mixtec, including their legendary hero Eight-Deer, who according to these accounts united all the Mixtec under his military rule until he was captured and sacrificed by his nephew.[11]

After the legendary departure of Quetzacoatl, the Toltecs continued to flourish at Tula for a time, through commerce. Despite the strength of the Toltec communities, migratory peoples from the north penetrated the region in the late 1200s and slowly became assimilated into this more sophisticated agricultural culture. One of these northern migratory groups, called interchangeably the Mexica or the Aztecs, arrived and generally resisted the Toltec way of life, except for their technology in warfare and agriculture. These people, who departed from a homeland in the north that they called Aztlán, had a warlike culture based on one of their principal gods, who required human sacrifice in return for their favors. According to the legend recorded in the Codex Azcatitlan.[12] These gods sent them migrating south, and they were to continue roaming until they received a sign that they had reached a new homeland.

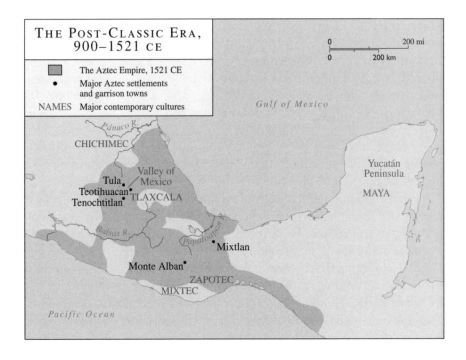

The Aztec Empire, 1521 CE

Major Aztec settlements
and garrison towns

NAMES Major contemporary cultures

For a time, the Aztecs and the Toltecs lived uneasily together in the region near the ancient, abandoned site of Teotihuacan. At one point the Mexica and one community of Toltecs prepared to exchange the daughters of two prominent leaders to seal an alliance through marriage. The Toltec woman who arrived in the Aztec community never became a bride. Instead, she was made into a human sacrifice. Outraged, the Toltecs gathered an army, drawn from many communities, and launched an attack on the Aztecs.

The Aztecs survived by fleeing to the major lake in the central valley, destroying what canoes they did not need, and paddling to an island for safety. Once there, they were dismayed by what they had done. Suddenly their path became clear. As told in their creation story, they received a sign when an eagle with a snake in its mouth flew into view and perched on a nopal cactus. Reassured by this divine omen, they began building a city that they called Tenochtitlán, founded, according to indigenous sources converted to the modern calendar, in 1325.

The Aztecs soon reestablished relations with the Toltecs and conducted regular patterns of trade. The Aztec population grew, thanks to improved diets based on intensive agriculture using terracing, irrigation, and floating barges. The typical Aztec relied on the diet of corn, beans, squash, and chilies, but enriched with avocados and other fruits and vegetables pictured in the codices. They found a rich protein source in chia seeds, so high in value that it became a sacrificial item as well as a major foodstuff. The rulers of the Aztec regularly had meat from deer or turkeys and enjoyed the rich, tasty drink, chocolate (created by grinding the bitter chocolate seed, adding spices to it along with boiling water, and frothing the mixture before serving).

As the population of the Aztecs grew, they developed extensive trade routes throughout central Mexico that brought a variety of goods, from the common maize to the luxury chocolate beans, to their capital. Along with trade, they expanded their realm through ferocious conquests. Merchants became the spies providing information to Aztec warriors, who undertook regular campaigns to expand their dominions. The Aztec system of empire building relied on battles in which the goal was not to kill the enemy but to take prisoners, who became sacrifices to the Aztec gods. This resulted in a different style of fighting in which they attempted to kill only enough of their enemies to intimidate the others into surrender. Prisoners joined the hundreds of people sacrificed annually.

The empire, which eventually stretched across central and southern Mexico, rested on the collection of tribute payments, and otherwise the conquered peoples were left largely on their own. The Aztecs made no effort to incorporate them by imposing linguistic or religious integration. The annual tribute payments typically consisted of corn, cotton blankets, and, occasionally, victims for sacrifice. In areas that produced a specialty product, that product served as the tribute to the Aztecs. Thus, chocolate-growing areas sent chocolate, regions with the exotic Quetzal bird sent the feathers, artisans who produced outstanding feather work sent their products, and areas that had rudimentary silver mines sent this precious mineral. Tribute records in codices survived the fall of the empire. The Spaniards, who came later and developed their own tribute system, often used these older records for their tax system.[13]

The wars increased the Aztecs' wealth based on the tribute they acquired. Through their centralized political system they ruled all of central Mexico as far north as settled communities existed, and south into the regions of the Zapotec (present-day Oaxaca). Throughout this area, the exchange was not all one-sided as they brought their sophisticated knowledge of architecture, agriculture, and government, including the use of the pictographs and the mathematics necessary for the keeping of records. Their wealth enabled the Aztecs to develop specialized occupations beyond food producers that other peoples could not, at least in similar numbers. They promoted both artists, including painters with a remarkable palette of colors, ceramicists, and poets, some of whose delicate, often despondent poems have survived.

The emperor Iztcoatl consolidated Aztec authority in 1430 by defeating the armies of Texcoco, a nearby rival town, at the battle of Azcapotzalco in 1430. He then standardized the religion and history of the region with his order to burn older codices and other pictographic histories because, he said, these accounts contained "falsehoods" contrary to the Aztec records. The Aztecs destroyed the accounts of the Texcocans as well as the Toltecs and other earlier peoples.[14] Over the next century, they created the most powerful empire in pre-Columbian North America, whose capital was one of the largest cities in the world at the time.

As their wealth grew, so did the size of the capital city, located on the islands in lakes of the great central valley. The Aztecs constructed causeways to regulate the lakes for irrigation and prevent flooding. They practiced a form of hydroponics on earth-covered rafts, or *chinampas*, which were called floating gardens by the Spaniards and later visitors to Mexico. The Aztecs made them by weaving "together the roots of aquatic plants, intertwined with twigs and light branches, until they had formed a foundation sufficiently strong to support a soil formed of the earth which they drew from the bottom of the lake." On them they grew "their maize, their chile, and all other plants."[15] The great central market far exceeded any other commercial center in the Americas, and it is estimated that the city's population reached 200,000 (with a million people in the central valley)—larger than any city in Europe, and perhaps in the world, at that time.

The Aztec peoples became increasingly stratified with a form of nobility at the top of society that combined both religious and military leaders, headed by a male emperor. Successful men had careers as warriors, priests, or, for a few, long-distance merchants, who also collected intelligence on prospective conquests. Women for the most part were responsible for child rearing and commonly worked in the fields that grew the foodstuffs for daily meals.

The Aztecs worshiped a pantheon of ferocious gods whose ceremonies were tied to the calendar. Often these deities appeared in different forms depending on the date. In addition to sacrifices, the critical element of their religion was the operation of the calendar that functioned much like the original Olmec system. It combined 20 day symbols (crocodile, death, money, vulture, wind, deer, grass, motion, house, rabbit, reed, flint, lizard, water, jaguar, rain, snake, dog, eagle, and flower), and thirteen numbers for the ritual calendar of 260 total days. They then combined the ritual calendar with an astronomical calendar used for agriculture and based on eighteen months of 20 days for a total of 360 days, with a 5-day dead period. The two calendars together created a fifty-two-year cycle.[16] The Aztecs considered the annual 5-day dead period and the end of the fifty-two-year cycle a time of danger. They held a religious ceremony of "The New Fire" with tremendous numbers of human sacrifices, based on their belief that only with sufficient offerings would the gods allow the world to continue. Archaeologists using skulls and skeletal remains combined with pictographic evidence have reconstructed these sacrificial ceremonies, with hundreds of victims.

The worship of these horrible and bloodthirsty gods makes the Aztecs difficult to understand. The most dominant was Huitzilopchlti, the god of war, joined by Coaticlue, the snake woman, and Tlaloc, the god of rain-

The Aztecs carved this twenty-five-ton, twelve-foot-diameter calendar stone in 1479. They arranged signs representing days in concentric circles around the face of Tonatuih, the god of the earth. The face was surrounded by an immediate ring cut into fourths that stand for the previous worlds. The Aztecs expected the fifth world, their own, to end as well. Additional rings indicated the days and years through signs and numbers. Scala/Art Resource, NY

fall. Only Quetzalcoatl, the god adapted from the Toltecs, had an avocation for various homey things (especially the drink pulque) and did not require sacrifices on a regular basis. This horrendous cost of lives found melancholy expression in the poetry and music that survive today. A few selections of the poetry have been translated into Spanish and English. For example, take this poem, known as "All the Earth Is a Grave":

> All the earth is a grave and nothing escapes it, nothing is so perfect that it does not descend to its tomb. Rivers, rivulets, fountains and waters flow, but never return to their joyful beginnings; anxiously they hasten on the vast realms of the rain god. As they widen their banks, they also fashion the sad urn of their burial.[17]

This poem, like most other examples of Aztec literature, has a somber quality and a preoccupation with death indicative of the Aztec belief that their world would end with the destruction of their society. Nevertheless, for most Aztecs not directly involved in the decisions of cosmology and conquest, life found satisfactions in close-knit family, familiar communities, and gratifying work growing crops or crafting useful items in beautiful ways.

Despite all the sacrifices that occurred, the Aztec religion predicted an eventual collapse of the entire society. Priests regularly examined omens and cast fortunes in an effort to foretell the coming of this end, perhaps with the return of Quetzalcoatl. In the year 12-House (1509), an increased numbers of omens appeared that seemed to foretell the end of the world. The wizards and diviners tried to interpret these ominous events, which included a weeping woman reported night after night by many residents of Tenochtitlan. Those who heard her told the wizards the woman wailed, "My children we must flee far away from this city."[18] Shortly, the end did come, but not as the Aztecs anticipated through their divination.[19]

Mexico's indigenous heritage is as rich and varied as the night sky filled with constellations, shooting stars, comets, and planets. The cultures, especially the earliest ones that seem lost beyond much recovery, have left vestiges that indicate their achievements in agriculture, astronomy, and architecture. Excavations of their pyramids, ball courts, and marketplaces have a magnetic appeal, drawing tourists and archaeologists the way they once drew the faithful members of the culture. These remains cannot completely portray the worlds lost long ago. For the Aztecs in particular, their world came undone not by their actions or the battles between gods but from decisions made in another world.

CHAPTER TWO

Conquest and Colony

In 1519, Hernán Cortés, commander of an expedition of a few more than 500 Spaniards and several Africans, in an act of mutiny ignored the orders of the governor of Cuba to abandon his exploring expedition and instead sailed from Havana for what we now call Mexico. First the expedition landed on Yucatán and then on the Isthmus of Tehuantepec, where they rescued one Spaniard from an earlier expedition who had been living with the local peoples and left another Spaniard behind because he had married into the indigenous community. Then, the conquistadors continued north along the coast, landed, and fought a pitched battle against the inhabitants. In order to reinforce peace after the combat, the native people, as was customary, presented Cortés with a young woman, called Malinche, who soon proved invaluable because she could translate the indigenous language. At first she had to speak with the repatriated Spaniard, but she soon learned Spanish herself and translated directly for Cortés. In this role as translator, Malinche has been portrayed as a traitor to Indian Mexico, and her name serves as symbol for betrayal of the nation to the present day.

Cortés arrived on the edge of the Aztec Empire in 1519 because of decisions made an ocean away in Europe. In 1492, Queen Isabella of Spain had financed exploration by the Italian Christopher Columbus to search for a western trade route to India. Instead he discovered the Americas. Isabella decided that Spaniards should conquer and convert to Christianity the peoples Columbus had encountered there. For twenty-five years, the Spaniards had focused on the Caribbean islands and nearby coasts. The governor of Cuba had planned to send an expedition to Mexico. He first offered the position to Cortés, then, deciding he did not trust this commander, tried to cancel the voyage. Cortés ignored the governor's cancellation and sailed for the coast of Mexico in 1519. Cortés, from Spain's central region of Extremadura, combined in equal measures daring, courage, and charisma that enabled him to inspire followers, intrigue strangers, and intimidate opponents. His superiors found him untrustworthy, his lieutenants unrelenting, and his opponents undaunted. He destroyed one world and created another.

Cortés, Malinche, and his expedition turned north along the coast until reaching the area of gold, where they founded the town of Veracruz, near the modern port of the same name. The local Totonaco people received the Spaniards with wonder and curiosity at the horses, guns, and bearded men. The Totonacos had been conquered by the Aztecs, so the local Aztec imperial lords sent messengers racing into the interior to report the Spanish presence to the Aztec emperor, Montezuma II.

Cortés's men, who had mutinied against the governor's authority, identified the people they encountered on the coast of Veracruz based on their expectations created by a casual knowledge of the Bible, travel accounts by Marco Polo and others, chivalrous novels, and the exaggerations, superstitions, and reports of previous expeditions around the Caribbean, such as the Grijalva visit to Mexico's Gulf Coast the year before (1518). The Aztecs, trying to understand who these visitors were, consulted their gods by reading auguries that confirmed their fatalistic expectation of a cataclysmic end to the world they knew and that explained the arrival of the surprise visitors.

Neither the Aztecs nor the Spaniards considered the other group exactly human, although they held rather different opinions. Some Aztec wizard-priests saw the Spaniards as gods, perhaps even Quetzalcoatl, the Toltec god who had departed with a promise to return; many Spaniards saw the Aztecs as some strange, pagan species, perhaps human and perhaps not. Later Spanish lawyers and clerics in a court hearing argued the case for and against Indian humanity that eventually resulted in the decision that Indians were human beings but with a childlike character.

Cortés, after some weeks, planned to visit the great Montezuma in his island capital, Tenochtitlan, on the site of modern-day Mexico City. Some of the Spaniards objected that in the interior they could be cut off and killed by the powerful Aztecs. Cortés settled the issue with the daring act of ordering the burning of the Spanish ships, dramatically committing the Spaniards irrevocably to march into the interior. With their guns, crossbows, and horses, the Spaniards were an imposing army. They fought several battles probably inspired by the emperor to test them as warriors, and after each one they obtained allies from the peoples who opposed the Aztecs. Notably, they reached an agreement with the Tlaxcalans, who had successfully resisted Aztec conquest. With these new allies, they ambushed and massacred the people of Cholula. The massacre transpired after Malinche reported to Cortés that the Cholulans planned to welcome the Spaniards and then kill them all.

Once the Spaniards arrived at the island capital, Cortés and the emperor met. Bernal Díaz del Castillo, one of Cortés's soldiers, years later wrote what he called *The True History of the Conquest of New Spain*, in which he described his first sight of the lord of the Aztecs. He recalled that after Montezuma stepped down from his litter, other great chiefs "supported him beneath a marvelously rich canopy of green feathers, decorated with gold work, silver, pearls, and chachihuites [jadite precious stones]." Montezuma's magnificent clothes included sandals, with soles made "of gold and the upper parts ornamented with precious stones."[1] At the meeting, both men adopted policies based on exigencies of the moment: the Aztec leader tried to appease the Spanish, including their obvious lust for gold and silver, and the Spaniard attempted to manipulate the emperor to mitigate the overwhelming numerical odds that might overwhelm the expedition.

For several days, the commander and the emperor cautiously negotiated and made efforts to intimidate each other. Spanish guns and horses astonished the Aztecs, and the Aztec numbers and weapons, especially the *macana* (a wooden sword whose blade was inlaid with razor-sharp obsidian), impressed the Spaniards, but it was the island city itself that overwhelmed their imagination. Cortés soon despaired, both out of fear they might never be able to escape the city and out of urgency to respond to reports of another Spanish expedition on the coast. Desperate to control the situation, Cortés seized Montezuma in an attempt to make him a Spanish puppet, placed a lieutenant in command in the city, and led an expedition carrying samples of Aztec treasure back to Veracruz to confront his newly arrived countrymen.

Facing Spaniards sent by the governor in Cuba to arrest him for mutiny, Cortés persuaded them to join his men in subduing the Aztecs and profiting from their treasure. His resolute actions were not matched in Tenochtitlan, where his lieutenant Pedro de Alvarado, misinterpreting a religious celebration as a military strategy, ordered an attack, killing the Aztecs gathered for the fiesta. The massacre turned Aztec leaders against the emperor and his captors.

Shortly after returning, Cortés attempted to use Montezuma to repair the situation, but this effort ended with the death of the emperor, as a mob of Aztecs angry with his appeasement policy attacked the Spanish position and Montezuma died in the battle. War followed, as the band of Spaniards and their Indian allies fought the warriors of the Aztec Empire. Battles continued for several months and were punctuated by atrocities, as the Spaniards tortured captives and the Aztecs sacrificed horses and conquistadors by beheading them or ripping out the hearts of prisoners taken in the fighting. With a population of several million as a source for warriors, the Aztecs far outnumbered the Spaniards and their Indian allies. Cortés, fearing defeat through attrition (he later wrote the king of Spain about the threat of an Aztec strategy of "removing the bridges at the entrances, and abandoning the place, they could leave us to perish by famine without our being able to reach the main land"),[2] decided on a daring night escape from the city. Bernal Díaz recalled the harrowing flight, in which they battled Aztecs both in front and behind them, and often in boats on both sides as they fled on a causeway from the center of the city. Eventually, the Spaniards escaped the city, but on this dreadful night more than 900 Spaniards, including five women, and at least a thousand Tlaxcalan allies died in the battle or as sacrifices.[3]

Cortés regrouped his surviving 400 men and about a thousand allies and developed a plan to subdue the city and the Aztecs. At the heart of his strategy was the construction of ships that could be used to patrol the lakes and lay siege to the city. Later, he wrote the king, "I made great haste to build four brigantines . . . large enough [for] three hundred men and the horses." Using these boats, he established a blockade that lasted weeks. The Aztecs had fresh water from one lake, but food became a problem. Moreover, the priests who performed daily auguries reported nothing but impending destruction of the empire. A surviving scrap of Aztec poetry expressed their despondent attitude and the desperate situation:

> We have chewed dry twigs and salt grasses;
> We have filled our mouths with dust and bits of adobe;
> We have eaten lizards, rats and worms...[4]

Under these conditions eventually the city fell to the Spaniards, and the Aztecs, whose religion had always predicted their destruction, nevertheless voiced their sorrow. The same poem captured their lament and defeat:

> Broken spears lie in the roads;
> We have torn our hair in our grief.
> The houses are roofless now, and their walls
> Are red with blood....
> We have pounded our hands in despair
> Against the adobe walls,
> For our inheritance, our city is lost and dead.[5]

The city fell to the Spaniards on August 13, 1521.[6] Because the victory occurred on the Day of Saint Hippolytus, he became the patron of the new Spanish city; a banner of green, white, and red dedicated to him was paraded through the city each year to celebrate the victory. The banner and colors would eventually become the flag of independent Mexico.

Cortés wrote Carlos V, the king of Spain and Holy Roman Emperor, to announce his victory, explain away his mutiny against the governor of Cuba, and proclaim his faithful service to both crown and church. In all, he wrote five letters to the crown. In the second letter he attempted to impress on the king the magnitude of his conquest by describing the Aztec Empire, its capital city, and its wealth.[7] As he described the city and its teeming population, he provided prospective by saying that of the many public squares, one was "twice as large as that of the city of Salamanca, surrounded by porticoes, where...daily assembled more than sixty thousand souls, engaged in buying and selling; and where [were] found all kinds of merchandise that the world affords, embracing the necessaries of life." Cortés alluded to Aztec natural wealth by enumerating the products in the market, especially "all kinds of green vegetables, especially onions, leeks, garlic, watercresses, nasturtium, borage, sorrel, artichokes, and golden thistle; fruits also of numerous descriptions, amongst which are cherries and plums, similar to those in Spain; honey and wax from bees, and from the stalks of maize, which are as sweet as the sugar-cane." Further enumerating their rich diet, Cortés listed the bread they made from maize, fish in many forms, paté of birds, and eggs. Beyond foods, the market held a great variety of cotton and other materials for making woven goods, that Cortés compared to the silk market in Granada. It also had pottery for a variety of uses including storage. Additional sections of the market had vendors of dyes and pigments for painters, and, on what the conqueror called an "herb street," others sold remedies and solvents that formed the basics of the medicine of the Aztecs. Moreover, he reported a surprising number of available services including barbers, restaurants, and porters.

Fine letter writing aside, Carlos V had no intention of allowing his new possessions in the Americas to remain in the hands of an adventurer who had ignored the royal governor and sailed to Mexico on his own initiative. The king planned on exercising his authority in Mexico to increase his personal political power, financial income, and religious reputation through missionary endeavors. In his kingdoms, because of arrangements made between Pope Alexander VI (a Spaniard) and Spanish monarchs Ferdinand and Isabella, the church, both its hierarchy and its missionaries, formed another of the Spanish royal administrative agencies. Crown authority over the church, called the Royal Patronage or Patronado Real, enabled the king, not the pope, to direct the church in Spanish lands.

Quicker than the arrival of the king's conquistadors, missionaries, or bureaucrats, European diseases swept through the indigenous population. Smallpox, pneumonia, and measles, previously unknown in Mexico, proved fatal to many Indian peoples. The death rates from those diseases exceeded those of the Black Death and other pandemics familiar to the Spaniards. The waves of these epidemics had severe effects in the society under construction by the Spaniards who occupied the capital. As death overwhelmed the indigenous peoples, it created the gloomy feeling of a ghost town in Mexico, despite the arrival of more and more Spanish men with a growing number of African slaves.

News, often exaggerated, about the conquest of the Aztecs inspired furious searches for even greater indigenous centers and their riches. These campaigns resulted in expeditions to the Andes and the eventual conquest of the Inca Empire, and in other expeditions in search of wealth. Some continued pursuit of a sea route to the riches of Asia, exploring north (Álvar Núñez Cabeza de Vaca's expedition to what is today the southeastern United States, and Francisco Coronado's search for the cities of Cibola, the cities of gold, in the southwestern United States), south (Pedro de Alvarado in Guatemala), and even an expedition (initially led by Alvarado) from Mexico's Pacific Coast to the Philippines. These expeditions often combined Spaniards with their Tlaxcalan allies, so that the people from what today is Mexico's smallest state left a cultural impact in northern Mexico, the southwestern United States, and the Philippines—including Tlaxcalan words in local languages. The conquest of Mexico inspired the conquest of Peru and the exploration of most of the Americas.

Missionaries, at first Franciscan monks, who were followed by members of the Dominican, Augustinian, and Jesuit orders, saw hundreds of thousands of souls to save everywhere in the Spanish dominions. Whether by design or, for the church at least, happy discovery, some missionaries found indigenous women to be faithful converts, who perhaps learned that Catholicism reinforced their domestic authority and particular relationships with males while offering them solace during their lives and promises of a better situation after. Depending on the mission, indigenous women found that both the missionaries and the crown backed them in various ways, ordering Spaniards to end the practice of living with several Indian women and directing

ycmoquayatcá que tlatoque

Franciscan missionaries baptized Indians, especially the leaders, giving them Spanish names after the saints to indicate their conversion to Christianity, based on modest instruction in the catechism. An Indian artist painted this baptism ceremony with the title "The lords have been baptized" in the Lienzo de Tlaxaca, a pictoglyphic history of the community on cloth, now lost. The version here has been re-created using images from a lithograph facsimile printed in 1892. The Mesolore Project, www.mesolore.net, Center for Latin American and Caribbean Studies, Brown University, and Prolarti Enterprises, LLC

them to marry women with whom they had established relationships. The importance of the Virgin Mary provided a significant role model, emphasized by both the missionaries and the new women converts.[8] In other regions, especially in the north, missionaries reduced the influence of women in communities and delayed communion for them.[9] They often reinforced patriarchal forms of the family.

As missionaries carried on their efforts to convert the pagans, Spanish entrepreneurs recognized the potential for huge profits from sugarcane, cochineal (a natural red dye), and tobacco. These men demanded land titles from the king and labor, at first Indian servants, and then African slaves. Beginning with Charles V, the Spanish crown ordered the registration of all migrants, to prevent ne'er-do-wells from polluting the colonial population. These registration records reveal patterns of migration and the most prevalent characteristics of the typical migrant. The Spaniards who went to Mexico were generally young, single males from Andalucia (the southern region of Spain that Queen Isabella, who had endorsed the early expeditions, directly ruled).

Beyond these general traits, the records reveal, understandably, that persons from different regions of Spain tended to follow relatives, friends, or at least people from the same community. As a result, some of the regional character, especially accents, music, and food, of the Iberian Peninsula became embedded in the larger American colonies and eventually Spanish-American nations; thus variants, for example, of Andalucian culture predominated in Mexico and of Extremadura in Peru. Moreover, Basque traders, although never a majority of the population, predominated in the merchant communities of many colonial port cities. They embedded their commercial skills based on family networks (including Crypto-Jews who used the networks to escape Spain for the colonies) in these communities.

The king soon appointed a brigade of bureaucrats to represent him in Mexico and in his growing American colonies. Of these colonial officials, the most prominent was the surrogate of the king himself, the viceroy. The office was first created in 1535 with the appointment of Antonio de Mendoza. The kingdom or viceroyalty of New Spain was divided into smaller units of different kinds involving judicial-administrative *audiencias*, military outposts as captaincy-generals, and strong community rule through city councils, called *cabildos* or *ayuntamientos*. The viceregal structure remained in place for just short of three centuries, that is, until the independence of Mexico in 1821. The regional administration was revised in the eighteenth century, but town government remained essentially unchanged. The viceroyalty of New Spain came to occupy an enormous region, with a northern boundary from California in a swooping line to Georgia's coast, Spain's Caribbean possessions, Central America, the coast of Venezuela, and the Philippines.

The confirmation of Spanish colonization, administrative units, and future exploration reflected the decision of Pope Alexander VI in 1493 to prevent conflicts between Spain and Portugal, the first European voyagers on a global scale. He divided the non-European world between them by creating a boundary line through the Atlantic Ocean and presumably around the globe at 370 leagues west of the Cape Verde Islands. The Spanish and Portuguese monarchs accepted the division in the 1494 Treaty of Tordesillas. The Portuguese received confirmation of their trading and slaving posts on the African coasts and commercial centers in the Indian Ocean and Far East. The Spanish crown received the Americas and some Pacific possessions, notably the Philippines. The line placed eastern Brazil and the South Atlantic in the Portuguese zone. Although both Spain and Portuguese generally adhered to this treaty, by the mid-sixteenth century, the English, Dutch, and French had rejected the division of the non-European world between the Iberian nations and sent explorers and pirates first and later colonists and navies to overthrow the Spanish and Portuguese monopoly.

The largest of all the European colonies, New Spain quickly proved to be the wealthiest, with its silver mines, sugar and tobacco plantations, cochineal dyes, and general agriculture. As such it received the special attention of the king. Wheat provided the basis of the Spanish diet and served as the only acceptable source for communion wafers. As significant as the introduction of wheat proved to be, bread did not replace the corn tortilla in the diet of indigenous and other commoners. The primary change in food for the native peoples was the introduction of chickens and pigs; their meals came to include eggs regularly and meat from both animals occasionally, resulting in altered and enriched diets.

Perhaps even more significant were the natural products from Mexico that enriched the diets in Europe. Corn became the basic food source for horses and cattle, while chocolate became a delicacy and tobacco an addictive pleasure. Other food products included avocados and turkeys. Peru sent potatoes, and the plantations on the Caribbean coast, the islands, and Brazil provided Spain, Portugal, and eventually much of Europe with both sugar and rum. Nevertheless, the basic diet in Mexico, with the addition of eggs, remained corn, beans, and chilies.

Spaniards, as agricultural producers and miners, demanded enough workers for their enterprises. The combination of declining indigenous population because of continuing epidemics and escalating efforts to mine silver and to produce commercial agricultural products resulted in major changes in the management of Indian labor. Over the first century following the establishment of colonial administration, the institutions governing the indigenous workforce changed three times.

First, the Spaniards followed the homeland pattern of social organization devised during the seven centuries of the Reconquest, when Spaniards fought to drive the Islamic invaders called Moors out of Spain, concluding in 1492 at the Battle of Granada. They placed Indian heads of families in trust to Spanish conquistadors and nobles, just as

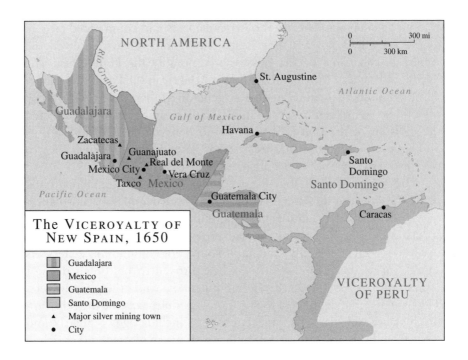

NORTH AMERICA

St. Augustine

Atlantic Ocean

Rio Grande

Guadalajara

Gulf of Mexico

Havana

Zacatecas

Guanajuato

Guadalàjara   Real del Monte   Santo
Mexico City   Vera Cruz   Domingo

Taxco   Mexico   Santo Domingo

Pacific Ocean

Guatemala City

Guatemala   Caracas

The VICEROYALTY OF
NEW SPAIN, 1650

☐ Guadalajara
☐ Mexico
☐ Guatemala
☐ Santo Domingo
▲ Major silver mining town
● City

VICEROYALTY
OF PERU

0 _____ 300 mi
0 _____ 300 km

surviving peasant families reclaimed from the Moors were placed in feudal fiefdoms for the Spanish officers and noblemen. Called the *encomienda* system in Mexico, it mirrored the peninsular feudal arrangement of theoretical reciprocal responsibilities. The Spaniards oversaw the conversion of Indian families and provided for their minimal well-being with food and housing. In return, Indian peoples supplied labor, tribute in the form of cotton blankets or special products such as honey or chocolate, and loyalty to their lords.

The *encomienda* system became the target of missionaries who became advocates for the Indian peoples. Most notably, Father Bartolomé de Las Casas denounced the violence of the conquest and the exploitation of the colonial system. His propagandistic argument addressed to the king, entitled *A Very Brief Account of the Destruction of the Indies*, described the situation in Mexico with these words in the introduction: "Their reason for killing and destroying such an infinite number of souls is that the Christians [the Spaniards] have an ultimate aim, which is to acquire gold, and to swell themselves with riches in a very brief time." He continued, "It should be kept in mind that their insatiable greed and ambition, the greatest ever seen in the world, is the cause of their villainies," and followed with examples of tortures and

This engraving of the Spaniards enslaving Indians illustrated the accounts provided in A Brief Account of the Destruction of the Indies by Padre Bartolomé de Las Casas. Such pictures created a general view of the brutality of the Spanish conquest in the Caribbean, Mexico, and Peru, that was used by England, France, and the Netherlands to justify attacks on Spanish silver fleets. Snark/ Art Resource, NY

cruelties that he swore he had witnessed. This and other similar accounts were obtained by imperial rivals and used as attacks on the Spaniards. These works circulated in translation served to create the so-called Black Legend of Spanish colonialism used to justify French, English, and Dutch attacks against the Spanish Empire.[10]

The barrage of contradictory claims and charges took some time to evaluate, but eventually the monarch decided to change the relationship between Spaniards in the Americas and the Indian workers. Although his explanations focused on the issues of Christian behavior, his actions revealed a concern with international diplomacy and his clear commitment not to allow the formation of an autonomous nobility with economic independence from his authority that a system of permanent indigenous peons might allow. His first effort ordered the abolition of the system by means of the New Laws of 1542. *Encomenderos*, those individuals who held the labor grants, collectively ignored the royal degree because it would leave them without workers unless they could afford to purchase slaves. Colonial officials in Mexico likewise made no effort to enforce the decree after learning that the viceroy of Peru's efforts to implement the law resulted in an uprising in which he was murdered.

The king's decree notwithstanding, the *encomienda* system ended when it no longer provided the labor necessary for agricultural production, especially of wheat, for the towns with growing Spanish populations. *Encomiendas* had been distributed as recognition of service to the crown or of noble status rather than specifically to those farming wheat. Faced with a system that no longer provided the workers necessary for the production of Spanish foodstuffs, the king in 1549 introduced the *repartimiento* system that recognized the significance of labor in the public interest. In practice this meant wheat production and silver mining across Mexico, and in Mexico City it meant work on the drainage system as flooding became an increasing problem in the colony's capital. In other colonies it often meant almost exclusively mining. Indian communities had to provide a fixed number of male workers each week; these men reported to a colonial official who divided them among Spaniards based on the area planted to wheat or the severity of the flooding. In mining regions, the workers went directly to the mines.

The system worked well as long as the population remained stable, but it did not. The number of Spaniards increased, and the number of Indians declined. Primarily disease, but also abuse and injury in the workplace, malnutrition (in some part caused by the elimination of *chia* as a major food item because of churchmen's belief that it was connected to blood sacrifices), and psychological depression all contributed to constant high death rates, in which some villages lost their entire population and in others it was greatly reduced. This forced labor system required communities to supply a fixed number of workers, so when the population declined, the labor demands became more onerous for the community. The *repartimiento* required workers to travel from their communities to a central location, and from there to an hacienda (plantation) or other work site. Travel exposed these workers to press gangs and robbers. Plantation owners soon complained to colonial authorities about workers who did not arrive. Officials in turn wrote the crown looking for a labor system that would provide needed workers and protect the individuals from attacks that destroyed any sense of personal security.

By the 1630s, the Indian workers subject to public service through the *repartimiento* suffered mounting insecurity because of epidemic diseases and other causes of population decline. Spaniards, in need of workers, or fearing they would soon be, became reluctant to trust the colonial officials to supply an adequate number of field hands. They turned to illegal ways of recruiting workers. Contract, or *gañan*, labor offered a solution welcomed by both parties. Hacendados (estate owners) gave contracts to workers that offered a small salary, a place to live, a patch for the family's subsistence farming, and protection from other labor contractors. In return, the hacendados got a reliable workforce. In this way, as the *gañan* system provided workers for large landowners, it also provided a more secure life for Indians for the first time since the conquest. With the emergence of this contract system, in 1632, the crown abolished the *repartimiento* system in Mexico.[11]

The search for personal and community security inspired some Indian leaders to master the Spanish legal and administrative system. This allowed them to utilize Spanish courts and the colonial bureaucracy to advantage. First, leaders turned to the legal system to conserve their lives in traditional fashion—their lands, their civic festivals, and their dress—insofar as possible by suing in the courts against Spaniards who came into their town to exploit the community or in efforts to regain lands taken from them. Second, community leaders recognized the legal protections given through municipal incorporation, so many sought and received incorporation as municipalities in which they preserved traditional governmental and economic patterns, including communal landholdings.

This mastery of Spanish law codes and bureaucratic procedures became a preoccupation of some indigenous leaders, who turned the legalistic colonial system to their account. The Spanish crown recognized the rights of incorporated local governments, whether they were Spanish or Indian communities, and protected them. Courts ruled against Spaniards who disrupted life in indigenous communities by trying to force them to sell their crops at ruinous prices, or pay imaginary taxes, or provide uncalled-for personal services. Judges sent them to fight on the northern frontier, ordered their transportation to the Philippines, or returned them to Spain. The crown increasingly recognized a responsibility to the indigenous peoples that included protecting them from unwarranted exploitation. The crown's concern showed clearly in the decision not to allow the Holy Office of the Inquisition to investigate Indians except in the cases of cannibalism and bigamy as well as a succession of court decisions to protect Indian community properties.

From Cortés's first display of cannons and horsemanship before Aztec officials when he arrived in Veracruz, the Spaniards used public rituals to demonstrate the authority of the crown and church, and to reinforce the social structure of the colony. These celebrations included the installation and funerals of viceroys and archbishops, swearing allegiance following the coronation of a new monarch, and various religious holidays. Nothing matched the celebration of Corpus Christi in Mexico City for pageantry and significance. This holiday quickly combined official and popular participants in the procession that moved from the cathedral on the central plaza, through the most important neighborhoods, and then returned to starting point. Location of groups in the parade made visible the social order and indicated the lockstep relationship of archbishop and viceroy and the prevalence of Christian religious beliefs for organizing the life of the colony.

The typical procession began with unofficial Indian dancers, as a metaphor revealing their presence in a society that officially gave them little place. Following the dancers came a large dragonlike float called the *tarasca* that expressed Christian views of sin and evil. The dragon, like the ones slain by Saint Michael and Saint George, appeared with seven heads that represented the deadly sins. The *tarasca* confirmed a social order of serious men, as it often featured as the rider of the dragon a woman or mermaid playing a guitar. This pictorial conflation of Eve from the Bible and the Sirens from Homer's *Odyssey* linked women, music, and sin. Following the dragon came the guilds, from the most common to the powerful silver workers, followed by religious brother- and sisterhoods from the most accessible to the most prestigious, schoolchildren, and government bureaucrats, religious orders and parish clergy, followed by the church and civil hierarchy. The archbishop with the host occupied the penultimate place and the viceroy, his retinue and body guards concluded the parade. The people of the community celebrated their beliefs and themselves, finding the significance of civil and religious institutions in the people who formed them.

At various points the parade halted with the host before a temporary altar, where some guild or confraternity had paid for a sermon combining praise for the church with that for the sponsor. Occasionally, these sermons through the use of puns and double meanings offered humorous or at least irreverent descriptions of colonial life. Often religious words were slurred together or separated to form the names of common fruit such as bananas, mangoes, or avocados in the communion or as one of the saints. Following the procession, the city enjoyed a major fair in the central plaza that by tradition offered new clothes (it is not clear if merchants sent advertisements and even sample clothes to the city's elite men, as they did in Madrid on Corpus Christi), among the myriad items on sale. Residents could use this and other fiestas to express piety, salute civil authorities, march with other social club members or use the opportunity to earn some money from their small businesses. When the parade and shopping ended, a festival followed with drinking, food, and a good deal of dancing to music disapproved by both the church and the government.[12]

With zeal matching that of the Spaniards seeking wealth through discovery, mining, or agriculture, the first missionaries worked feverishly to salvage the souls of people they considered to be indigenous heathens. In 1521, twelve Franciscan missionaries (a number sent in honor of Jesus and his loyal disciples) walked into Mexico City. Cortés expressed their significance when he received them by dropping to a knee and kissing the hems of their robes. Evangelization under the Franciscans resulted in mass baptisms and giving Spanish names to indigenous peoples. All the major religious orders soon sent missionaries to compete in these evangelization campaigns. Once Ignatius Loyola and his followers organized the Society of Jesus, the Jesuits (as they were called) swarmed into Mexico to convert and educate the native peoples as well. Leaving aside the niceties of the Roman Catholic faith, the missionaries rushed to save souls by baptism, signaling conversion. Only the Dominicans approached conversion from the opposite position, delaying baptism until the prospective convert had some knowledge of the catechism.

The long-standing efforts included the use of dramatic performances, dances, and fiestas to make biblical and Christianization stories come alive in the indigenous imagination. How much the indigenous peoples appropriated Spanish Catholicism and used it as a cover to continue their own beliefs and how much the indigenous and European religious practices resulted in some combination of both religions remains unclear. Certainly some Indians identified the Christian Trinity and saints with the Aztec gods, and church leaders reported the continuation of Aztec religious practices, even some sacrifices. One hypothesis argues that indigenous peoples mastered a system of parallel religious practices and the ability to switch codes of behavior as it was necessary. Whatever the situation, the population of Mexico became and remains, at least in name and outward practice, Roman Catholic.

The most dramatic and enduring event of the evangelization era was the miracle, if one is a believer, of the appearance of the Virgin of Guadalupe. The legend reports the appearance of the Virgin to an indigenous shepherd boy, Juan Diego. Juan Diego reported it to Archbishop Juan Zúmarraga, who dismissed it as the hyperactive imagination of a recent convert and asked for indisputable evidence of the miracle. The Virgin appeared three more times to Juan Diego, and twice more the archbishop rejected the story. During the Virgin's fourth appearance, she had the boy take roses wrapped in her cloak to the archbishop. The cleric opened the cloak to discover not the roses Juan Diego expected but instead the image of the Virgin emblazoned on the cloak. The Virgin in this avocation appeared with physical features similar to the indigenous peoples, with coarse dark hair, dark eye color, and dark pigmentation.

Following this appearance on December 12, 1531, the cult surrounding the Virgin of Guadalupe grew slowly for a few years and then became more important. Today skeptics point to some evidence that the cloak was painted with indigenous pigments by a member of the Indian painters' guild called Pablo. Nevertheless, now the Virgin is the patron saint of Mexico and of Latin America. The image of the Virgin, along with the eagle, is the ubiquitous and popular symbol of Mexico.[13]

From the first landing of Cortés, the Spaniards experienced one surprise after another in Mexico. The crown, in order to protect the indigenous peoples from the shoddy religious behavior and moral turpitude of many of the Spaniards, issued decrees meant to structure life in his colony. Of these efforts, the most sweeping was a law to create a society divided into two parts: the Republic of Spaniards (la república de los Españoles) was supposed to consist of the Spaniards and their African retainers and slaves; the Republic of Indians (la república de los Indios) was supposed to include only Indians. The two groups were to live separately. Spaniards and Africans were prohibited from spending the night in indigenous communities, and other visits from merchants and labor organizers were severely restricted. A second decree regarding marriage also aimed to maintain the separate societies and regulate immortal behavior. All Spaniards with wives in Spain were ordered to bring them to Mexico, or face deportation. Single Spaniards living with Indian women were ordered to marry the woman or end the cohabitation.

Despite these efforts, the surprise for the crown and royal officials came with the appearance of two large populations they had not anticipated. First, the African population grew more quickly throughout the colony than anyone expected. In tropical agricultural zones and urban centers, African slaves and freed peoples outnumbered the Spaniards. Second, despite the efforts to keep Spaniards and Indians separate, many of the largely male Spanish arrivals developed relationships with

Indian women. This occurred in such high numbers that there quickly emerged a population of mixed ethnicity, generally called *mestizos*, that also outnumbered the Spaniards and who, for the most part, wanted to be recognized by their Spanish fathers. Many were not, and they became a resentful population that eventually would threaten colonial rule. These included the predominant patriotic commander from 1811 to 1815, Padre José María Morelos.

The ethnic intermixing soon included the African population as well. Overzealous Spanish bureaucrats eventually concocted a table of ethnic types called *castas* that divided the New Spanish population into sixteen groups based on ethnicity. Artists in the eighteenth century soon painted pictures to provide the royal court and the curious in Spain with an image of the different castes, their pigmentation and dress. The colonial society designed only for Spaniards and Indians became a curious mix of ethnicities in which an individual could pass for a member of different categories based mostly on his clothing and language. Mestizos usually adopted Spanish clothing, especially trousers and jackets, and women wore skirts and blouses; Indians, at least cultural ones, continued to wear shirts and pants of native cotton (or, later, muslin) without buttons, and ponchos rather than coats, and the females wore *huipils*, one-piece smocklike dresses, or skirts with poncho-like tops. The inability to speak Spanish marked the indigenous communities.

Mexico City, within a century of the conquest, became one of the world's largest cities—more populous than any in Europe, with an overlay of educated individuals and sophisticated institutions above a sea of ethnicities characterized by poverty and poor health. The capital boasted a university (a century before Harvard), a newspaper, a book publisher, and a cadre of polyglot individuals, including playwrights and composers.[14] In the midst of wealth and luxury expressed by the viceroy, the archbishop, and the colonial court, the poor, ragged population, the incessant flooding, the periodic disease epidemics, and occasional grain shortages rivaled the disparities of wealth that characterized such cities as Paris, London, and Madrid.

Among capital city elites of the late seventeenth century, the savant nun Sor Juana Inés de la Cruz stood out for her poetry and religious exercises. Many consider her writings to be the beginning of Mexican literature. She taught herself to read, write, and do arithmetic, and during her teenage years she mastered both Latin and Nahuatl. She entered a convent in 1667 and two years later became a regular member of the Order of Saint Jerome. As a nun she wrote devotional studies and literature, including satire, and took an interest in science. Her work was widely read in Spain as well as in Mexico, where she was praised as the Tenth Muse. In 1690, a letter to the viceroy attacked her interest in science as opposed to theology. Sor Juana replied in the "Response to Sister Filomea," a statement in favor of women's right to education. For this action, the archbishop condemned her willful behavior and forced her to give up her scientific and literary activities.[15]

The desperate conditions of many people notwithstanding, the city had a cosmopolitan character as the center of the far-flung of colony of New Spain. The colony reached west across the Pacific to the Philippines, and the connection was maintained largely through the annual voyage of the Manila galleon, a massive ship that traveled from the islands to Acapulco and returned, starting in 1565. The galleon became the sailing ship of legend, a huge mahogany vessel packed with Asian spices, silks, ceramics, and occasionally slaves. Captains made enough money to retire after a single four-month voyage. Capturing the Manila galleon became the dream of every pirate, and two British buccaneers, Francis Drake and Thomas Cavendish, did so and were knighted for it. Generally the ship eluded the pirates and overcame bad weather to arrive with the Asian goods that became fashionable in the capital city. The galleon hauled back Mexican silver pesos that soon became the common trade currency in Asia from China to East Africa.

The world's richest colony faced major changes when European wars, concluding with the War of the Spanish Succession in 1713, and royal dynastic changes enabled the Bourbon family to replace the Hapsburgs. The Bourbons, with French and French-trained advisers, introduced Enlightenment practicality, with its emphasis on efficient programs of civil government, public health, and tax collection and with goals of tightening political authority and revenue collection in the colonies, especially New Spain. These reforms were analogous to programs introduced in the Portuguese (the Pombline reforms) and British colonies (the Granville reforms).

In one of the most dramatic steps, Carlos III ordered the expulsion of the Jesuits, whom he regarded as a threat to his authority from Spain and the colonies in 1767. This was paired with political and economic reorganization handled by the all-powerful inspector general, José de Gálvez, who attempted to streamline colonial administration and economy as he liberalized trade and introduced enlightened practices of health and agriculture. The independently organized Sociedades Económicas del Amigos del País became centers of enlightened practices, promoting such practices as smallpox vaccinations.[16]

Miners and merchants benefited most from the Bourbon reforms. But when Napoleon placed the Spanish king under arrest and invaded and occupied a portion of Spain in 1808, the merchants' profits were threatened. They began to consider their situation. Many discovered they had a stronger commitment to their native land of Mexico, its peoples and its prospects, than to Spain and its monarch, caught up in European affairs. These Spaniards born in New Spain (called *creoles*), the mestizos, and other castes with this glimmering of national aspirations began to consider independence. Once again decisions in Europe shaped events in Mexico.

CHAPTER THREE

Independence and Its Challenges, 1810–1844

In a remote village, miles from the viceregal capital, a priest, a captain, and a councilman held a desperate meeting on September 15, 1810. These three rather ordinary men had plotted an uprising to gain independence for Mexico. Just recently they had learned that their conspiracy had been betrayed. Their plans and their predicament resulted from faraway events in Europe and changing circumstances in New Spain. Fearing they would be arrested and even more concerned that their goals would be thwarted, they faced the decision of their lives.

New Year's Day of 1800 introduced a new century and brought a feeling of dread about the future of their world to many people in the colony of New Spain, especially to those who called themselves Spaniards, whether *peninsulares*, that is, Spaniards born in Spain, or *criollos*, or creoles, that is, Spaniards born in New Spain. Their anxiety came, above all, from the rise of the French empire, built on the foundation of the revolution of 1789 and the ambitions of Napoleon Bonaparte. They recognized the prospect of yet another war, doubted Spain's ability to defeat the French alone, and worried about an alliance with Great Britain, their long-standing enemy.

Apprehension about dangerous European possibilities soon became reality. Napoleon created the French empire and embarked on the conquest of neighboring countries. In 1808, he decided to weaken Great Britain by attacking its long-standing ally Portugal. Because the British controlled western Europe's seas, the French field marshal planned an overland invasion to cross through Spain and then sweep into Lisbon. Napoleon called the Spanish king to a meeting at the French-Spanish border to discuss his troop movements. Once both leaders had arrived, Napoleon in quick succession ordered the arrest of the Spanish monarch, forced his abdication in favor of his son Ferdinand VII, placed the latter under house arrest, and named his own brother, Joseph Bonaparte, the new king of Spain. He commanded French troops to march into northern Spain and from there to invade Portugal.

Ferdinand VII's subjects throughout the Spanish kingdoms, including Spain's colonies in the Americas, rejected French rule and determined to fight for their king. The Spanish loyalists, joined by colonial volunteers who relied on guerrilla warfare, successfully prevented the occupation of southern Spain. Colonial loyalists, anticipating French efforts to claim Spain's far-flung colonial territories, organized patriotic societies to defend their homelands.

Patriots in New Spain appeared quickly and varied greatly. Some, especially in Mexico City, met to express their loyalty to Ferdinand VII. Others swore allegiance to him but debated the colonial relationship to Spain and even the monarchy itself. A few demanded the creation of a crown regulated by a new constitution that would make colonials equal to Spaniards. At the same time, a few others, doubting Ferdinand would ever recover the throne, argued for independence. The patriotic society in the town of Querétaro, with members from throughout the Bajío (Mexico's north central region), became the most insistent that New Spain break its ties to French-dominated Spain.

Several Querétaro society members concluded that independence offered the residents of New Spain substantial benefits. Among the most outspoken were the three obscure men, the priest, captain, and councilman: Padre Miguel Hidalgo, Captain Ignacio Allende, and Councilman Juan Aldama. They argued that breaking ties with Spain promised increased home government, celebration of Mexico rather than its denigration as a colony, greater individual opportunity, and promotion of practical, useful knowledge over spiritual commitment and hierarchical loyalties with little reward. Broken down into specifics, home rule meant officials would consider Mexican needs first and that tax money would stay in Mexico. Celebration of the country meant replacing Spanish condescension with pride at being born in Mexico. Removal of foreign preferment meant the political, economic, and social benefits so often given as rewards to Spaniards would go to those who earned them. In place of concerns with loyalty to the crown and adherence to the faith, independence would result in the promotion of useful practices such as vaccinations and road building. Padre Hidalgo went further, suggesting independence should mean the end of head taxes and labor drafts to work on Mexico City's drainage or silver mines demanded from Indians and African peoples,. He urged the distribution of land to the lower groups in society. Within the patriotic society of Querétaro, these goals received various degrees of support, but a majority favored self-rule. The members of the patriotic group conspired to declare independence.

Throughout 1810 rumors traveled in and out of Mexico City's colonial and church offices, coming and going from the patriotic societies and administrative meetings. This intelligence gathering on both sides relied on women, whom men often dismissed as innocuous; thus they had access to many confidential conversations and documents. For the patriots, one of the most active women was Doña Josefa Ortiz de Domínguez, wife of a former official in Querétaro. Casual gossip and verified information about independence conspiracies startled colonial officers, who determined to arrest the conspirators. Hearsay about these government decisions rebounded in the other direction and soon reached Querétaro, where Doña Josefa sent messages to the leaders of the plot, Captain Allende in the town of Guanajuato and Councilman Aldama in the town of San Miguel El Grande. The news and the arrest of several of their coconspirators sent both men to the village of Dolores to consult with Father Hidalgo.

Hidalgo pressed the others to reach a decision during the night of September 15. After discussion of their reduced options, all three concluded—with varying degrees of eagerness—that they had to call Hidalgo's parishioners to arms against Spanish authorities before everything was lost. Before dawn of September 16, Father Hidalgo rang the chapel bell, calling his parishioners to church, where he inspired them to rebellion in the name of Our Lady of Guadalupe in order to end bad government and expel the Spaniards from the country. According to an artful reconstruction of his speech from various recollections of people there, he supposedly cried out:

> My children: a new dispensation comes to us today. Will you receive it? Will you free yourselves? Will you recover the lands stolen three hundred years ago from your forefathers by the hated Spaniards? We must act at once.... Will you defend your religion and your rights as true patriots? Long live our Lady of Guadalupe! Death to bad government! Death to the Spaniards![1]

With these words, Hidalgo and his companions mobilized a haphazard group of parishioners, many of whom were in town to celebrate the village's saint day. Instead of joining the festivities, several musicians, for example, joined the insurgents. The patriots set off to fight against the Spaniards in the nearby town of Guanajuato. On the way to San Miguel El Grande to collect volunteers, the motley group stopped at the hacienda and monastery of Atotonilco, where Hidalgo slashed the image of the Virgin of Guadalupe from its frame to use as their standard.

Padre Miguel Hidalgo, father of Mexico's independence, initiated the struggle for freedom from Spain in the early morning of September 16, 1810. The image is widely used because it shows a white-haired, honest-faced individual, suggesting wisdom, experience, and openness to others. Hidalgo had earlier promoted the planting of grapes, raising of silkworms, beekeeping, leather tanning, and brick making to increase the income of the Indians near his small town of Dolores, Guanajuato, now named Hidalgo in his memory. Library of Congress, LC-DIG-ppmsc-04595

News of the uprising quickly reached Guanajuato, the main regional center. Spanish authorities and their sympathizers decided to defend the town from the fortresslike public granary. The two-story stone building built around a large central patio appeared impregnable against the rebels, who had no artillery and were armed with only a few muskets and pistols, but mostly machetes, slingshots, and homemade pikes. As the rebels approached, the Spaniards and their supporters and their families flocked into the granary seeking protection from the approaching mob from the countryside. Hidalgo's men put the granary under siege. They identified the building's wooden gates as its only weak points, but this was less of a weakness than it first appeared. As several of Hidalgo's men soon learned, the defenders could shoot at or pour scalding water on anyone approaching the gates.

Quick thinking offered a solution. One of the rebels retrieved a gravestone from a nearby cemetery, placed it on his back for protection as he crawled up to the granary, and started a fire to destroy the gates. Known as El Pipila, or turtle man, because of his protective shell, he has become a hero in elementary schoolbooks, and today his statue towers over the town. Once the burning gates fell, Hidalgo's army surged into the building, where they murdered most of the adults, including women, and looted the building, the dead, and the survivors for anything worth taking.

The rebels continued southward toward Mexico City. They seemed all the more dangerous for their appearance—disorderly, unmilitary, almost like refugees as they herded appropriated livestock for their commissary, carried home furnishings as their plunder, and dressed in outlandish combinations of peasant clothes and looted finery. Hidalgo himself had put away his priestly garb in Dolores, according to anonymous contemporary description, for "ankle boots; purple trousers, blue sash, scarlet waistcoat; a green coat; a black ruffle and collar; a straw-colored kerchief around his neck; a turban with plumes of every color except white; [and] a Moorish scimitar at this waist."[2] To many in New Spain, Hidalgo's insurgents were not an army but a mob, with no higher goals and no better practices than the pirates they looked like.

The rebels advanced on the colonial capital, but once they reached the edge of the valley containing Mexico City, Hidalgo ordered them to turn northwest toward Guadalajara. His decision not to attack the capital has never been well explained. Whatever his reasons for turning away from Mexico City, Hidalgo understood where victory lay. He knew that the Spaniards had to defeat him and his men, whereas his victory required only that he keep an army in the field. Nevertheless, the decision to turn away gave the Spaniards an opportunity to organize their campaign against Hidalgo.

The fierce General Felix Calleja took command of Spanish and local loyalist forces. He instinctively devised techniques to defeat Hidalgo's forces by adopting a scorched-earth antiguerrilla campaign. He ordered the execution without trial of anyone taken prisoner in battle or suspected of fighting with Hidalgo. He commanded the burning of homes and fields and the confiscation of animals and crops of anyone who, willingly or not, supported the rebel priest. This ruthless policy soon took a toll as Hidalgo's forces began to melt away, many trying to return home to Guanajuato province. Calleja also proved his ability as a battlefield commander at Puente de Calderon, outside Guadalajara, where Hidalgo's depleted army made a stand. The Spanish general's men won a decisive victory.

The loss to Calleja after ten months in the field persuaded Hidalgo to divide the survivors into guerrilla bands under trusted leaders, while he and his advisers attempted to reach Louisiana in search of volunteers and aid from the United States. Hidalgo, Allende, and Aldama nearly managed to reach the Rio Grande before they were captured and taken to the district capital of Chihuahua City. Colonial officials immediately tried and convicted Allende and Aldama of treason, while Hidalgo faced the Inquisition court, which sentenced him to death as well. Firing squads executed the three rebels. Then their corpses were beheaded. Spanish authorities ordered the bodies buried in Chihuahua and the heads taken to Guanajuato City, where they were placed in iron cages and hung on the corners of the granary, the site of their early victory, as a public warning.

The guerrilla bands created by Hidalgo continued to fight. In the south, another priest, Father José María Morelos, took command. He sent home anyone who did not have a horse, gun, and sword. The remaining men formed a mounted and well-armed troop. Morelos proved an adept commander during the next four years as his rebel army struck quickly, won small battles, and disappeared. With this strategy, the rebels soon controlled a large section of central Mexico.

During these same years, the insurgents' circumstances in New Spain, including the question of the king, were changing in response to events in Europe. Defenders of Ferdinand VII, seeking a unified campaign against the French, in 1811 called for an assembly of elected representatives from throughout the realm (including the colonies). The delegates met in the city of Cadiz in southern Spain, which remained free of French troops. The representatives, including fifteen from New Spain, formed a congress, called a Cortes, that expressed their loyalty to the crown. They then undertook the writing of a constitution for all the kingdoms. Mexican delegates came and went from Spain but generally participated actively on committees and in debates and voted with the majority to create the 1812 constitution. This document, which later served as a model for liberal regimes throughout the nineteenth century, from Greece to Russia, created a constitutional monarch who answered, especially in finances, to the assembly of elected representatives from the entire realm. For Ferdinand VII's subjects outside of Spain, the constitution offered not home rule but local self-rule through municipal government.

The constitution called for the invigoration and expansion of municipal councils in Spanish lands. This provision directed the incorporation of local governments in every settlement with at least 1,000 people. Giving communities legal status created locally chosen municipal officers who had authority over local lands, taxes, and militia service. In this way, the delegates in Cadiz shifted governmental decisions about everyday life to local communities. This decision decentralized government and, in the minds of many, made independence from Spain irrelevant.

The fighting in New Spain destroyed the ability of colonial institutions to operate across the viceroyalty. Decentralization followed, with local authorities, including local army units, exercising independent actions. Hidalgo's creation of several guerrilla groups had moved Spanish officers to respond with divided, largely independent commands. For the remaining years of the decade, violence had a local focus rather than grand campaigns for independence, loyalty to the crown, or Mexican home rule. Just as often the fighting expressed rivalries grounded in every possible social division: village against village, Spaniard against creole, Indians against outsiders, well-to-dos against ne'er-do-wells. In this era of sporadic and seemingly chaotic warfare, rumors had a great hold on the people of New Spain. They widely accepted stories of Ferdinand VII traveling across Mexico in a closed coach, which allowed individuals to fight for independence from Spain, not against the king who had supposedly joined them in Mexico. Other common rumors included those of Indian hordes rampaging across the country intent on re-creating the Aztec Empire by slaughtering all Europeans, and of a mestizo outlaw gang whose leader planned to make himself king.

Even the defeat of Napoleon at Waterloo in 1815 and the restoration of Ferdinand VII to the Spanish throne the same year did little to end the fighting or to re-create central authority in New Spain. Reinforced and rearmed Spanish troops successfully defeated and executed Morelos in 1815, but this did not deter dozens of other local commanders who remained in the field. Instead, a kind of normal life developed, especially in the countryside, with naturalized violence that included periodic warfare with sporadic raids, violent attacks, looting, banditry, and death. Local warlords, in the name of Spanish officers or independence commanders, held sway in most regions across Mexico.

These local captains found opportunities to promote their own careers and enrich themselves by riding the ridges of their territories. They collected fees for crossing their districts, ran protection scams to guard the properties of the well-to-do, and sold escort services to travelers. Both the restoration of colonial authority and the creation of an independent nation threatened these lawless local bosses.

Uncertainty and ambition created the circumstances that ultimately ended Spanish rule. Colonial officials, especially Viceroy Juan O'Donojú, a Spanish nobleman of mixed Irish-Spanish heritage, who had been ignored by both Spaniards and insurgents, became increasingly concerned that the colony would collapse from decentralization or would be invaded by foreigners, particularly the British, or overwhelmed by a popular uprising of native peoples, perhaps as had happened with slaves in the Haitian Revolution (1791–1794). This uncertainty led men working in the viceroyalty's government to search for a solution to the fighting and a way to restore central government. Meanwhile, the ambitions of a onetime Spanish officer turned regional warlord, Agustín Iturbide, made him zealous in his search for opportunities for colony-wide authority. He seized on the insecurities of colonial administrators to propose to various loyalist and insurrection leaders a peace agreement. At a meeting in Cordoba, Veracruz, several prominent leaders signed a treaty that did not threaten their authority, promising that an independent Mexico would respect the church and seek a European monarchy. Iturbide offered all the residents of New Spain his Three Guarantees of independence, equality, and religion.

The fine print for each of the Three Guarantees had deeply conservative references. Independence was explained as the creation of a Mexican kingdom with a European monarch, perhaps even Ferdinand VII himself; Equality (sometimes by early historians stated as Fraternity to echo the French Revolution) removed all ethnic designations, calling residents Americans, but in practice only ensuring equality of Spaniards and creoles; and Religion guaranteed that the Roman Catholic Church would remain as the only institution of the faith tolerated in the new kingdom.

The Three Guarantees offered little enough change that they were able to attract widespread support among loyalist and insurgent leaders, who felt confident their local commands were secure. On this basis, the Army of Three Guarantees faced almost no opposition as it marched to Mexico City. In the central plaza, with little thought to future danger or the challenge of realizing his promise, Iturbide declared the fulfillment of independence on September 27, 1821.

The aftermath of independence resulted in an elected congress charged with creating a constitutional monarchy and identifying a European king or prince willing to come to Mexico to rule the new nation. The first proved easy and the second difficult. After some eighteen months, delegates learned that no European prince wanted to come to rule Mexico, a country that Ferdinand VII stated he would reconquer and return to his realm. Bewildered by these setbacks, delegates lacked direction. Popular demonstrations by veterans of the independence army in the capital's streets suggested a solution.

Veterans of Iturbide's Army of Three Guarantees began to march through the streets demanding that their general be named emperor. Enough evidence exists to identify Pío Marcha, Iturbide's sergeant major, as the organizer of these demonstrations but not enough to conclude, despite good reason for the suspicion, that he acted with the encouragement of the general himself. Veterans gathered outside the residence of Iturbide and demanded he assume the title. Later, they pulled him in his carriage to the assembly's meeting to discuss the possibility. They packed the galleries, where they clicked their swords within their scabbards to drown out anyone speaking in opposition. In this way, the military dictated the creation of the First Mexican Empire with Iturbide as emperor in 1822.

Agustin and his wife, Ana María, crowned emperor and empress in borrowed jewels and rhinestones, produced the glitter of royalty. But they could not rebuild the shattered Humpty-Dumpty colony of New Spain. This onetime member of the king's men struggled to rule with dignity, initiative, and imagination.

He soon received diplomats from the United States and Great Britain, who were motivated to visit by commercial plans and curiosity about Spain's former colony. The acerbic South Carolinian Joel Poinsett had little but contempt for both the emperor and his new nation. His hostility focused on what he saw as the rhinestone glitter of Iturbide's court and the emperor's reputation. He wrote about Iturbide, "His usurpation of the chief authority has been most glaring, and unjustifiable; and his exercise of authority arbitrary and tyrannical." He added, "I will not repeat the tales I hear daily of his character." During the struggle of independence, he was "accused of being the most cruel and blood-thirsty persecutor of the patriots." Then of course he changed sides. His biting commentary showed clearly in his judgment of the working classes. He wrote, "They are sober, industrious, docile, ignorant and superstitious; and may be led by their priests, or masters, to good or evil."[3] Despite his minister's hostility, President James Monroe extended diplomatic recognition. The British quickly followed suit, offering recognition and sending as their first representative Henry George Ward, Britain's first diplomatic representative in Mexico with the title of minister of Great Britain. Poinsett and Ward represented rival nations and belonged to rival Masonic lodges. They competed savagely in efforts to build up trade with Mexico and promote their versions of Masonry. For Iturbide, diplomatic recognition provided almost his only success. Nevertheless, Ferdinand VII refused to recognize Mexican independence and maintained troops on the island of San Juan Ulloa, which controlled access to the port of Veracruz. He constantly presented his plans to reconquer the country in his official statements on Mexico.

Building on the diplomatic recognition that welcomed Mexico into the family of nations, Iturbide sent representatives to Europe in search of 30 million pesos in bank loans to rebuild his nation's economy, especially to restart silver mining and pay the nearly 3 million peso deficit in government expenses for 1822. An Englishman of doubtful background offered 10 million pesos in loans, but the loan failed when Mexicans wanted evidence that he actually had the bank's money before signing any papers. Additional unsuccessful efforts in London, Paris, and Washington, D.C., pushed Iturbide to print paper money that quickly declined in value. In this way, Iturbide initiated financial practices that set Mexico on the path of devalued currency and foreign debts that has been typical of the nation's history.

Diplomatic recognition notwithstanding, the crippled economy intensified the localism of regional leaders. Filipinos and Central Americans declared their independence from Mexico, and the state of Chiapas departed to become part of Guatemala. Other remote provinces, especially Yucatán, California, and Texas, had only tenuous ties to the empire, suggesting that the new nation might collapse in pieces. Moreover, Ferdinand VII continued to announce his intentions to reconquer the former colony.

Faced with mounting difficulties, Iturbide needed the company of soldiers to help hold things together. He also looked to churchmen, who could use the pulpit to promote popular support. Most critical, he needed economic recovery. He relied heavily on miners and planters, who could restore exports. He obtained the backing of only a few men from each of these groups. Not many trusted him. Many more saw him as a freebooter captain (while fighting with the royalists, he was relieved of command in 1816 because of charges of embezzling army funds, creating commercial monopolies, and collecting protection fees) whom luck had made emperor, a position his merits had not earned and his talents could not manage.

The emperor's collaboration with chance lasted barely ten months. Army officers and congressmen conspired to bring down the regime they had helped create. The officers issued a statement called the Plan of Casa Mata, according to custom named for the location where it was proclaimed. The plan had the barest of goals, stating only that the officers intended to end the empire and establish a republic. Iturbide could offer little to build support beyond invented titles, such as commander in the Order of Guadalupe, which meant little. Therefore, as his loyal troops dwindled, he was forced from office and sent to an Italian exile with his family. The first empire ended.

A liberal interlude from 1824 to 1833 followed the expulsion of the emperor. Liberal Mexicans based their programs on reducing the role of the Catholic Church in everyday life; restricting the privileges of churchmen, military officers, and large landowners; and creating a republic rather than a monarchy. Their first step was to write the constitution of 1824, largely modeled on the Spanish constitution of 1812 but with the critical difference that it established an elected president and congress. The particulars of the executive office, its term, and duties somewhat resembled those of the United States, and the voting, also like that of the United States at the time, was indirect and highly restricted. Nevertheless, in a popular choice, the independent General Guadalupe Victoria won the first presidency.

Often criticized for the limited successes of his government, Victoria served out his term, until 1828. The survival of the administration, despite deep political rivalries and an armed rebellion, should not be undervalued. Between 1828 and 1876 only one other president managed to serve his entire term. The former emperor, always looking for opportunities to regain his position in Mexico, reappeared during Victoria's administration, returning to organize a defense against a rumored Spanish invasion. When he arrived in 1824 near Tampico, Iturbide was arrested, tried for treason, and executed in accordance with a congressional law that stated he would be shot to death without trial if he ever returned.

After Victoria's presidency, the republican experiment began to encounter opposition, especially from church leaders and conservatives who favored some form of authoritarian rule. The republicans also battled among themselves, as the intensity of politics made compromise nearly impossible. Disputed elections and attempts to create military dictatorships added political disruption to the economic difficulties that plagued the nation. The threat that these conditions made to the survival of the nation seemed clear in two foreboding episodes.

The first was the Spanish invasion in 1829 near Tampico. Young commander Antonio López de Santa Anna developed a strategy, helped by his familiarity with the tropical lowlands of Veracruz. He kept the Spanish pinned down, allowing yellow fever and malaria to take their toll, rather than have his troops attack the invaders. The army mobilization in response to the Spanish invasion aggravated the social and economic disorder common throughout the republic. The other ominous episode resulted from the overturning of the second president, Vicente Guerrero, in 1830. Forced from office by his vice president, Anastasio Bustamente, and conservative military officers, Guerrero fled to Acapulco in his native province (today the state is named for him). In the port city, Guerrero arranged passage into exile on an Italian ship, the *Colombo*. The ship's captain had already negotiated with the Bustamante government for a bounty, if he should capture Guerrero. As soon as the former president boarded the ship, he was overpowered, bound hand and foot, and shipped to Mexico City. Captain Picaluga received 50,000 pesos (equal to dollars at the time) for Guerrero, who was tried for treason and executed on January 14, 1831.

These events seemed to foretell an ill future of foreign invasions and military takeovers with deadly consequences for Mexico. The events also discredited Bustamante, who ordered the execution of Guerrero and popularized Santa Anna, who had defeated the Spanish. With acclaim as the savior of the nation, Santa Anna won election as president in 1833.

Santa Anna and his vice president, Valentín Gómez Farías from the north, seemed to be the first executives who shared the same political vision to build a more secular society with limitations on both the church and the military. Almost immediately, Santa Anna retired to his Veracruz hacienda, pleading ill health, and leaving Gómez Farías to initiate the reforms. Most historians think Santa Anna wanted to see the popular reaction to these reforms before being associated with them.

Gómez Farías believed a republican society required the reduction of the presence and the influence of both the military and church in everyday life. His reforms included minimizing the size of the army and the jurisdiction of separate courts for the military, and removing education from church direction. Among the specific actions to achieve the latter, the government closed the University of Mexico, whose faculty were almost exclusively clergy. Other reforms made paying the church tithe a religious, not a national legal, obligation and allowed both monks and nuns to abandon their vows and return to everyday life.[4]

The response was both predictable and prompt. Church and military leaders protested the assault on their privileges in society. Under a banner of "Religion and Fueros" (institutional privileges), these rebels called for the overthrow of the Santa Anna–Gómez Farías regime. This revolt against elected government acquired a comic opera character when the rebels took Santa Anna prisoner and only freed him when he agreed to lead them against his own government. This action better than any other demonstrates Santa Anna's almost magical charisma. Over and over in his career he changed his politics, disappointed his followers, and then charmed them again. His love of racehorses and fighting cocks made him a friend of sporting men, while his gallant manners and graceful dancing made him appeal to women. He appealed to ordinary army recruits, as a soldier's soldier. He remains the enigma of nineteenth-century Mexico. Santa Anna toppled the republic in 1835 and established a strongly authoritarian regime based on a charter of seven principles, called as a result the Sieta Leyes (Seven Laws). Curiously, even with the collapse of the republic, prominent Mexicans found reasons for optimism about their country.

Intellectuals found encouragement, notwithstanding political instability, in widely distributed scientific reports and newly compiled statistical tables. These scholars, army officers, and amateur social reformers drew inspiration from two European scientists, Alexander von Humboldt and Adolphe Quetelet. Humboldt traveled from 1799 to 1804 throughout Spanish America, spending the year from March 1803 to March 1804 in New Spain. Eventually he published thirty volumes by 1834, and sixty-nine by 1870, describing physical geography, plant and animal life, resources, and peoples. In the volume *Political Essay on the Kingdom of New Spain* (1811, in French), he poured out his praise for Mexico's potential because of its natural bounty of precious metals, growing population, fertile lands, and favorable location that only needed to be developed. Mexicans would long share Humboldt's conclusion that they were living in a treasure trove.

Quetelet in the 1820s turned his scientific research from astronomy to Parisian society. He developed what he called social physics in a search for natural laws of human behavior. He compiled statistical tables to show birth, death, and literacy rates; frequencies of crime, including

More than any other Mexican in the first forty years after independence, General Antonio López de Santa Anna captured the public and political imagination. President, dictator, and uncrowned king, he led his country eleven times; in war commanded Mexican forces against the Texans, the French, and the United States, and was forced out of office and into exile. He remains an enigmatic figure because of his brilliant charisma and shocking failures. Library of Congress, LC-USZ62-21276

prostitution; and disease. He concluded that the calculations in these tables revealed Parisian identity as distinct from universal human nature. Building on Quetellet, French scientists soon organized a national society of geography and statistics that served as the model for similar groups in England, Germany, and other European countries. Mexican intellectuals soon followed the French example, producing statistical tables and in 1833 organizing the National Institute of Geography and Statistics.

José Gómez de la Cadena, in 1839, published a study of population statistics in the institute's first bulletin. He examined Mexico City's birth, death, literacy, crime, and disease rates and compared them with similar information for London and Paris. The comparison enabled him to draw the shocking conclusion that Mexicans lived longer, safer, and more literate lives than Londoners and Parisians, described in their statistics and the novels of Charles Dickens (in *Oliver Twist*) and Victor Hugo (in *Les Miserables*). Humboldt identified the wealth of natural resources, and Quetellet's methods revealed the wholesome, healthy population. Thus, Mexican intellectuals concluded their nation was, indeed, a land of promise.

For all these promising statistical tables, Mexicans recognized dangerous social conditions. The long struggle for independence and the seemingly endless political upheavals prevented reestablishment of many economic activities. Banditry flourished in this disorder. The lack of social stability caused political breakdown as well. Several states, especially Yucatán, withdrew from the union for various periods. On one occasion, Yucatán, linked by the wind and water currents in the Gulf of Mexico to New Orleans, unsuccessfully sought annexation to the United States. Widespread political and social disorder attracted foreigners who hoped to profit from the nation's apparent weakness. Two major threats to national existence came in the 1830s, with the Texas Rebellion and the first French intervention.

A complex combination of motives resulted in the settlement of Texas by U.S. citizens, pulled by land at cheap prices and the promise of adventure and pushed from the United States by debts, crimes, or narrow opportunity. These settlers formed a community of sorts with the Mexicans who had arrived for the same reasons. Together these Texans and Tejanos (Mexicans in Texas) revolted in order to leave the strongly centralized government created by Santa Anna.

Santa Anna's new government in 1835 eliminated much self-government and imposed taxes on the settlers of the province in the far north. Santa Anna centralized the regime and replaced elected state governors with appointed department heads. Almost immediately, state leaders revolted in Yucatán, Texas, and the silver mining zone of Durango in the name of the Republic of the Sierra Madre, named for the local mountain range. Santa Anna decided to lead an army north to put down the Texans, and, by making an example of Texas, he hoped the other independent states would return to the union.

Santa Anna's army advanced into Texas without opposition until it arrived in the mission town of San Antonio. There a few more than 150 Texans and Tejanos had taken up positions in an old mission called the Alamo (named for the nearby oak trees). Colonel William B. Travis commanded the defenders and, recognizing an overwhelming mismatch, tried to negotiate an armistice. Santa Anna, mindful of the the need for an example, refused to consider anything except an unconditional surrender; he wanted a battle that would reverberate in the Sierra Madre and Yucatán. His buglers blew the charge without quarter, and Mexicans swarmed over the fort, eventually killing most of the defenders. The handful of Texans who surrendered were promptly executed without trial. Besides Travis, the dead included folk heroes Jim Bowie (for whom the knife is named) and Davy Crockett. Santa Anna and his men quickly marched on to the nearest Texas garrison at Goliad. Here the defenders, remembering the Alamo, accepted Santa Anna's demand for unconditional surrender. Santa Anna, after collecting their arms, ordered all 240 men executed for treason.

Sam Houston, who commanded the remaining forces in the field, had no intention of fighting a battle against the Mexicans. He hoped evasion would keep the rebellion alive. Santa Anna's troops were soon on the heels of Houston's men but could not corner them for battle. The two armies shuttled across central Texas, with Houston often ordering his men to double-time to stay ahead of Santa Anna's pursuers. Finally, at San Jacinto, today in greater Houston, the Texans camped, in near exhaustion. The Mexicans bivouacked to recover their strength. The Texan pickets noticed that Santa Anna failed to post guards and roused Houston, who ordered all his men to attack Santa Anna's camp. In a battle lasting less than half an hour, the Texans defeated the Mexicans, took several hundred prisoners, and began to collect scattered soldiers who had escaped.

Among the prisoners, the Texans identified General Santa Anna. Houston seized on the situation to compel Santa Anna to sign treaties ending the fighting and recognizing the independence of Texas. Despite some sentiment to execute the prisoners of war in memory of those killed at the Alamo and Goliad, Houston agreed with Santa Anna that the prisoners would retreat south of the Rio Grande, well below the traditional Texas boundary of the Nueces River. The retreat of the Mexican forces quickly became the basis for the Texan argument that the Rio Grande was their boundary.

Houston, personally taken with Santa Anna and his willingness to negotiate, arranged for the Mexican general to go to Memphis to meet the vacationing president of the United States, Andrew Jackson. Jackson, in turn, shared pleasant discussions on horse racing and cockfighting with his prisoner and arranged for the U.S. Navy to deliver Santa Anna back to Mexico at Veracruz. Once he returned, Santa Anna learned that the Mexicans believed he had betrayed them by signing treaties that recognized the independence of the northern state. His countrymen soon sent Santa Anna packing into exile.[5]

Almost before Mexicans could take in the events in Texas, they faced another threat to their nation. Ambition drove the newly restored French king, Louis Philippe, in his search of national glory. Mexico seemed a promising adversary because of its incessant political upheavals and economic miseries. These very problems also provided a motive to make demands on the Mexicans. The French had a fascination with Mexico that prompted artists, entrepreneurs, scientists, and confidence men to go there. Soon, many of these adventurers had lost money or property through unpaid loans, damage from military takeovers, and endemic banditry. They appealed to the French government to help them obtain financial settlements. In 1838, Louis Philippe seized what he saw as an opportunity and sent a fleet to demand that the Mexican government pay $600,000 pesos in claims. Mexican officials reviewed the claims and discovered one submitted by a French baker, who reported Mexican troops had broken into his shop and helped themselves to more than 100 pesos' worth of pastry. The Mexicans still mock the French by referring to this episode as the Pastry War.

As the French had anticipated, Mexicans refused to pay the claims. The French cruisers dispatched troops who took the city of Veracruz and held hostage the Mexican port and the commerce that passed through it. Finally, the Mexican Congress agreed to arrange payment, but the French added the sum of $200,000 pesos as a collection fee for total claims of $800,000. In response, the Mexicans declared war and named Santa Anna as the commander to undertake the defeat of the French army, demonstrating again the belief that he was their best general, even if politically unreliable.

The fighting lasted barely a month and was limited to the city of Veracruz. Santa Anna personally led his troops and in one battle received wounds that forced the amputation of his left leg just below the knee. The ferocity of the Mexicans persuaded the French to accept the Mexican promise to pay $600,000, and they withdrew their troops on March 9, 1839.

Santa Anna again captured national attention, this time as a hero who forever would suffer from wounds received as a national sacrifice.[6]

He did not have to wait long for an opportunity. He regained the presidential office in 1842 and used his authority to arrange a lavish state reburial for his left leg, brought from Veracruz and placed in a monument in Mexico City. The ceremony involved the congress, cabinet, diplomatic corps, and church leaders. Those in attendance could not know that even greater sacrifices would be demanded of the country's leaders.

Numerous explanations have been given for the instability of Mexico that invited foreign intervention and encouraged even more domestic political upheavals. These conclusions range from the political inexperience of the people as a result of the heritage of colonial authoritarian rule to the hyperpolitics that resulted from the newness of the political experience, to the social explanations including illiteracy and ignorance that created a gullible population susceptible to demagogic caudillos (charismatic leaders, usually military men, typical in nineteenth-century Latin America). Beyond these cultural-political explanations, leaders shared an experimental approach, developing hypothetical governments such as a monarchy, republic, and dictatorship, almost without attention to the nature of the society.

Perhaps a good part of the answer for these experiments rests with individuals who dominated the country after independence. For example, the first generation of commanders of the army in 1840 included 118 senior generals and colonels, all of whom had fought in the wars of independence. Of the total, 25 were Spanish born, and 81 were creoles who had served in the Royalist Army during the struggle, and only 12 officers had fought for independence.[7] These men accepted independence rather than lose their country, but they favored and fought for a form of government that guaranteed their military privileges, prestige, and social stability. Similar personnel patterns existed in the other major institutions, the church and the bureaucracy especially. Thus, both the unwillingness to experiment and the lack of widespread support for new governing institutions, especially republican constitutions, become understandable.

The heads of the parish priest, the army officer, and the city councilman hung on the corners of the granary at Guanajuato from 1811 until 1823, when the military commander Anastasio Bustamante ordered them taken down. In 1824, the men who created the first republic had the skulls from Guanajuato and the remains from Chihuahua brought for reburial in Mexico City. In 1895, the remains of these leaders were interred in the monument to independence (called the Angel) on the most important street, La Reforma Boulevard, in the capital city. They remain there today.

CHAPTER FOUR

Embattled Mexico,
1844–1876

Neither the Texas war nor the Pastry War, although humiliating for national leaders, especially Santa Anna, changed little in the country. Texas remained a distant wasteland, and the Texas regime a pasteboard republic. The French received some money and more promises, but Mexicans still had access to European loans, and the mining industry had begun to recover. Certainly, the national regime faced problems, particularly a Maya uprising called the Caste Wars in Yucatán and the peninsula's constant secession from the Mexico City regime. Nevertheless, the nation seemed as secure as many in Europe and more so than the Central American republics.

Everything changed with decisions made in the United States. James K. Polk, elected president in 1844, made a commitment to territorial expansion and determined to oversee the creation of a transcontinental nation. In short order, the U.S. Congress annexed Texas, and Polk dispatched diplomats to London to resolve joint control over the Oregon Territory that stretched from Alaska to California, and to Mexico City to purchase ports on the Pacific Coast that would benefit New England maritime merchants. England and the United States agreed to a treaty that divided Oregon at the present U.S.-Canadian border, but Mexican officials expelled the U.S. representative, making it clear they neither accepted the loss of Texas nor planned to sell any ports in California. Polk immediately began searching for a provocation for a declaration of war.

After considering what Mexican actions might justify invasion for some weeks, he confided in his diary a request to Congress based on the hostile treatment of his emissary, the bellicose statements in regard to Texas, and the general disrespect for U.S. territorial claims. On May 9, 1846, he discussed this "ample cause for war" with his cabinet, all of whom supported him, except for Secretary of the Navy George Bancroft. Polk worried congressmen would see his statement for what it was, a request to declare war because of impolite behavior and bad manners.[1] Events in the Rio Grande valley, a region claimed by both Texas and

Tamaulipas, saved him from this indignity. A messenger arrived that same evening with reports of an exchange of gunfire between U.S. and Mexican troops that resulted in some casualties. Polk demanded a declaration of war to retaliate against what he framed as Mexicans "shedding American blood on American soil," a phrase that quickly became the rallying slogan of the pro-war faction and the sarcastic commentary of opponents, such as Abraham Lincoln.[2]

The U.S. Congress declared war on Mexico in April 1846 in a close vote, with the opposition coming from the party out of power, including Abraham Lincoln, who denied the skirmish had occurred in American territory, and others who opposed the conquest of any territory that might become slave-owning states. The latter concern led Free Staters and abolitionists in western New York and Ohio to lead demonstrations against the war and oppose military conscription and budgets throughout the struggle. Despite this opposition in the North, militias from Illinois and other midwestern states served. Southerners generally supported the war and used names of battles to name towns such as Buena Vista, Alabama; Saltillo, Mississippi; and Mexico, Missouri.

The U.S. intervention took place in three areas: the invasion from Texas into northeastern Mexico; a march from St. Louis to Santa Fe, New Mexico, that divided, sending some troops south into Chihuahua and others west to California; and the principal invasion, an amphibious assault under the command of General Winfield Scott at Veracruz that involved marines, regular army, and militias. This force, following Hernán Cortés's route of conquest, fought a series of battles (Cerro Gordo, El Molino del Rey, and Chapultepec) that led to the occupation of the capital city.

Santa Anna, despite his bravado during the Pastry War that provided him with the popular acclaim again to occupy the presidency, had been forced into exile in Havana when rivals overthrew his government to establish a regime committed to reclaiming Texas. Following the U.S. declaration of war, he contacted President Polk with an offer, if transported to Mexico, to resolve the war. Polk doubted that Santa Anna would negotiate the peace terms he wanted, but he decided that the exile's return would disrupt the Mexican war effort, so he obliged. Back in Mexico, Santa Anna took command of the Mexican troops. Santa Anna fought General Zachary Taylor to a draw at Buena Vista in the north but lost the major battles for the center of Mexico (Cerro Gordo and El Molino del Rey). Nevertheless, he successfully kept an army in the field and, in the losses, avoided having his army destroyed. Technology created the disparity: Mexican soldiers carried

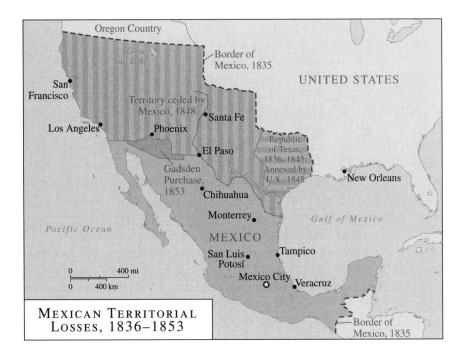

**MEXICAN TERRITORIAL
LOSSES, 1836–1853**

the barrel-loading muskets of the Napoleonic Wars against U.S. troops armed with breech-loading rifles that fired ready-made cartridges. The difference in weaponry gave the United States a three- or four-to-one advantage in firepower.

Technology changed other features of warfare. Samuel F. B. Morse's invention of the telegraph created a more rapid means of communication. Journalists, sending reports to the closest telegraph station in the United States, seized on the technology to provide more frequent and more timely battlefield reporting to the United States and beyond. The recently invented daguerreotype resulted in battlefield photographs. The United States–Mexican War was the first war to be photographed.

Even as they lost battles in this war of aggression, the everyday Mexican defenders defined patriotism and bravery and paid in blood for their rights as citizens. The defining episode of patriotism came when Santa Anna determined quite correctly that the capital could not be defended and that attempting to do so would result in tremendous civilian losses. He led his surviving troops out of the city. At Chapultepec, the military school, the remaining cadets, all too young to serve on active duty, decided that national honor required them to defend the city. They battled the advancing U.S. Marines until only six cadets remained, and these valiant defenders took down the national flag, which one wrapped about his shoulders, and they all plunged to their death from the fort's parapet. The cadets have been honored by the U.S. Marines in the first line of their hymn ("From the Halls of Montezuma") and by the Mexican government with statues and plaques as the Boy Heroes, but their most enduring monument comes from the people, who recognize that they have defined valor and patriotism for as long as Mexico stands.

Equally courageous guerrilla bands based on local militias sprang up to ambush, cut off, disrupt, and generally harass the U.S. troops. In some cases, no doubt, communities turned to veterans of the independence wars for either leadership or lessons for survival in the chaotic situation that followed the destruction of government. By the end of the war, Scott's army had been stretched to near the breaking point in its efforts

THE STORMING OF CHAPULTEPEC SEP: 13ᵀᴴ 1847.

This painting depicts the advance of U.S. Marines against Mexico's national military school called Chapultepec, on September 13, 1847. Their victory completed the conquest of the capital city and ended formal resistance in the U.S.-Mexican War. The school was defended by cadets too young to be called into regular service. These "Boy Heroes" remain the most heroic defenders of the nation, commemorated in monuments at the entrance to what today is Chapultepec Park. After James A. Walker, The Storming of Chapultepec, Sept. 13th, 1847 *(1848), chromolithography with applied watercolor, 23 9/16 x 35 15/16 in., Amon Carter Museum of American Art, Fort Worth, Texas, 1974.48* to protect supply lines and maintain even a semblance of control in the conquered regions. The militiamen and the communities that supported them, including the women who provided food and provisions, acted according to their sense of civic life, that carried with it both rights and responsibilities. Guerrillas and soldiers continued to fight for another ten months in the ebb and flow of violence that allowed for neither victories nor defeats. They fought and waited for the politicians to pronounce an end to the war that in a real sense had already ended.

The Treaty of Guadalupe Hidalgo signed on February 2, 1848, concluded the war. Its provisions forced Mexico's leaders to recognize the loss of Texas and the loss of the so-called Mexican Cession (New Mexico, Arizona, California, and most of Nevada and Utah)—together representing approximately half of the nation's territory. The treaty obligated the United States to provide citizenship and protection of property of those Mexicans living in the annexed territory. Article VIII of the treaty read, in part, "Property of every kind, now belonging to Mexicans,...shall be inviolably respected. The present owners, the heirs of these, and all Mexicans who may hereafter acquire said property by contract, shall enjoy with respect to it guarantees equally ample as if the same belonged to citizens of the United States."[3] This provision remains a major issue that has resulted in numerous court cases, especially concerning title and use of land and water in the U.S. Southwest, particularly New Mexico.

In the treaty, the U.S. government assumed $3 million in U.S. claims against the Mexican government and paid $15 million in reparations. Nicolas Trist, who negotiated the treaty for the United States, believed the demands had been too harsh on the Mexicans but nevertheless pushed ahead with the agreement. The treaty ended the war, but more than anything else, it shaped the course of politics for the rest of the century.[4]

As a derelict nation for the next three decades, Mexico survived the trauma, but barely. The U.S. military occupation increased the sense of vulnerability, and the massive loss of territory in the north eliminated the territorial cushion between the victor and the vanquished. The U.S. border had moved closer to the heartland and might well move again, perhaps eventually extinguishing independence. Both Liberals and Conservatives concluded they faced a task of regeneration. The liberals approached the task as an economic more than political crisis. A backward nation lost the war, as many understood, to military technology and organization. Modern weapons, military engineering, communications, and logistics made the difference. José María Mata, the principal author of the constitution of 1857, had been a prisoner of war (captured at the Battle of Cerro Gordo), and while a captive in New Orleans, he had studied the enemy at close range. He argued that Mexico could appropriate parts of the U.S. model. Other liberals, even during the U.S. occupation, made some tentative reforms at the municipal level as they struggled to salvage the country from further dismemberment.

The sting of defeat and the loss of territory motivated a national search for an explanation for the internal causes. The Conservatives, in particular the acerbic Lucas Alamán, explained the tragedy as the only possible outcome once the new nation abandoned its heritage of hierarchical rule under a monarch, the legacy of Spanish culture, and the social cement of the Catholic Church. To ward off a predatory United States, he and other Conservatives advocated the establishment of a monarchy allied with European powers. As incentives, the Mexican monarchy could offer access to mineral wealth and a market for European manufactured goods. Economic concessions in return for mutual defense characterized the approach. Antipathy for monarchy as a protective device encouraged the Liberals to turn to the United States as a model and for assistance.

Despite his party's contrary view on monarchism, the Liberal Miguel Lerdo de Tejeda worked together with the Conservative Lucas Alamán to develop political and economic strategies for yet another Santa Anna regime. They agreed on Lerdo's proposal for a Ministry of Development in 1852 to foster industry and railroads for economic growth. Their collaboration also called for renewed efforts to attract immigrants. Conservatives, of course, wanted only Catholics, while the Liberals preferred northern Europeans, mainly Protestants, who they believed had superior industrial and technical skills.

A gaggle of Conservative presidents held office, as Conservatives tried to mobilize support for a monarchy and a few others plotted to find a European prince who would come. Neither group had much success, nor were they discouraged. Undaunted by these developments, Alamán forged a regime led by an uncrowned president for life. He chose Santa Anna, bringing him back from yet another exile, for the position. Moreover, he dismissed the need for a constitution or charter for the regime, arguing that "Santa Anna, well advised," would suffice, making clear that he would serve as adviser. Santa Anna, who had been forced into exile again after the U.S.-Mexican War, returned from his Long Island, New York, banishment and began creating a court decked out in green and gold, regal in every way except for a coronation.

Alamán as Santa Anna's minister of foreign affairs explored alliances with European nations with mild results. France sympathized but was unwilling to jeopardize its trade with the United States. Spain discussed the idea of a secret mutual defense pact with Mexico as a way of protecting Cuba. On second thought, the government in Madrid remembered the difficulty of keeping secrets and decided that such a pact might provide the pretext for U.S. seizure of Cuba. A Mexican approach to Prussia to secure military training failed. When events, particularly the U.S. Civil War, changed the international equation, obstacles to European interest in Mexico evaporated. Meanwhile, Alamán died, and Santa Anna would tolerate no other adviser. Santa Anna's attempt to use colorful ceremony and elaborate ritual to build acceptance of, if not loyalty to, his new regime would not be sufficient.

Santa Anna, personal ambition aside, was a committed patriot. One of his contributions to the nation came in the form of the national anthem. The president, with the urging of the members of the well-known literary society the Academy of San Juan de Letrán, and several composers, in 1853 announced a contest for the best poem that could serve as the words for a national anthem. When poet Francisco González Bocanegra won the contest, Santa Anna immediately opened a second contest for composers to write music for the words. Jaime Nunó won. Nunó, a Catalan musician, had directed the Queen's Regiment Band in Cuba from 1851 to 1853 and had come to Mexico at the invitation of Santa Anna. Nunó's music and González Bocanegra's words were heard for the first time when the soprano Balbina Steffennone and tenor Lorenzo Salvis sang the new national anthem at the Santa Anna Theater as part of the Independence Day celebration, September 15, 1854. The composer, during a period of civil war, fled to Buffalo, New York, and his song also fell from grace. The Liberals who came to power in 1855 opposed the song as the music of Santa Anna. Nevertheless, it continued to be played and sung at the grassroots level and in the 1870s reemerged as the national anthem, with increasing popularity. Nunó, teaching piano and writing brass band music, knew nothing of this until the Pan-American Exposition of 1901 in Buffalo. The Mexican Army Band, attending the world's fair, went to Nunó's house and played the anthem in an appeal for him to return to Mexico. The composer remained in New York but made two tours of Mexico and on one of them presented a march in honor of Porfirio Díaz. Following his death in 1908, he was buried in Buffalo, but in the 1940s, Mexican President Manuel Avila Camacho arranged for him to be disinterred, brought to Mexico, and reburied in the rotunda of illustrious persons next to the poet and lyricist González Bocanegra. At times, some individuals have tried to change the anthem. At one point, it was even translated into the Aztec language, Nahuatl. Finally, Congress passed a law stating that it could not be changed.[5] These are the lyrics in English translation:

Mexicans, at the cry of war,
Prepare the steel and the steed,
And may the earth
Shake at its core
To the resounding roar
Of the cannon.
Gird, O country, your
Brow with olive
The divine archangel of peace,
For your eternal destiny
Was written
In the heavens by the
Hand of God.
But if some strange
Enemy should dare
To profane your ground
With his step,
Think, O beloved
Country, that heaven
Has given you a soldier in
Every son.

The phrase "mas si osare" (But if [some strange Enemy] should dare) in the second verse is often sung, especially by schoolchildren, as "Masiosare," playfully making the phrase into the name of "some strange enemy." Popular singer-songwriter Chava Flores includes this name in a list of new given names for children reflecting world events in his song "Vámos al parque, Céfira." The anthem stands as one of Santa Anna's greatest contributions to the nation.

Liberals explained the political debacles of the first half of the century as the result of vestigial colonial institutions. The church hierarchy and the feudal estates, the great haciendas, in combination, kept the people in superstitious ignorance and grinding poverty. *Moderados* (moderates) saw collaboration with the ruling group as possible, while the *puros* (radical liberals) opposed Santa Anna. Along with some colleagues, Benito Juárez, the young governor of Oaxaca, went into exile in New Orleans. He worked in a cigar factory while others worked on the docks. Plotting their return, they charted a new course for economic vitality for the republic with technology and transportation as the keys.

Railroads, roads, and even canals became topics considered in Liberal newspapers. Collecting the newest gadgets and machines became somewhat of a liberal hobby for exiles in the United States or visitors to Europe.

Ignacio Comonfort, Melchor Ocampo, and José María Mata all bought Isaac M. Singer's advanced sewing machines (invented in 1851) the moment they became available and brought them back to Mexico. Liberal travelers, returning home, often filled their trunks with promotional literature on railroads, factories, devices, medicinal cures, and inventions. Francisco Zarco, one of the leading Liberal journalists, reminded his fellow Liberals, who dreamed that technology would change everything, that only political stability offered the social circumstances that would allow for economic development. For Zarco, political stability could only be achieved with a separated church and state and general education for the people. He regularly issued pamphlets that repeated his views.[6]

Liberals found complementary opinions about technological and transportation expansion in the United States, particularly in the South, centered in the commercial hub of New Orleans. In general, southerners believed their region had become an internal colony of the wealthy, industrial North. A business conference in Montgomery, Alabama, in 1858 suggested that Latin America offered economic opportunities for the South. New Orleans's *DeBow's Commercial Review* advocated a Tehuantepec railway to link the port of New Orleans, some 700 miles to the north, to a Mexican port on the eastern terminus of the proposed railway, then across the narrow isthmus to the Pacific and on to Asia's markets. The Gulf of Mexico properly envisioned would become an American lake. The desire to paper over sectional conflict linked these fantasies with national political opinion.

Significantly, the last territorial loss for Mexico, achieved through the U.S. Gadsden Purchase, involved a plan to build a transcontinental railroad from New Orleans to California's Pacific coast. The discovery of gold in northern California added an additional attraction. U.S. Army surveyors decided that the most accessible route for a railroad lay just south of the newly established national border, in Mexico's Mesilla Valley. How much land might be necessary seemed unclear, and instructions to the U.S. minister and railway promoter James Gadsden left the issue open. The original treaty between the United States and Mexico on December 30, 1853, agreed to a $25 million purchase price for this part of Mexican territory, with $5 million held back to settle claims, and it included navigation rights in the Gulf of California. After the

Senate rejected the treaty, a strong reaction at the commercial convention held in Charleston, South Carolina, rallied southern and western support and forced it through the Senate on April 25, 1854. The price offered dropped to $10 million for much less land than Gadsden had in mind. In addition, it provided for right of passage across the Isthmus of Tehuantepec. Santa Anna's desperation for money to finance his regime led to his reluctant acceptance of the price, and ratification by the U.S. Senate followed on June 30, 1854.

The Mesilla Treaty, or the Gadsden Purchase as it is known in the United States, provided the last straw to opponents of Santa Anna. As further fuel for their objections, instead of a focus on development President Santa Anna appeared more interested in creating and maintaining a court with regal trappings. A calendar of court-centered events and holidays preoccupied Santa Anna and suggested a drift into monarchy. His newly organized bodyguard, modeled on that of Emperor Frederick William, dazzled many spectators with their green-and-gold uniforms and blond hair and whisker wigs. Perhaps more important, Santa Anna ignored Liberal politician Lerdo's advice on a reasonable trade policy, raising tariffs and making arbitrary changes in customs regulations, but allowing his close supporters special import and export privileges. A navigation act of June 1854 abusively taxed foreign ships entering ports with goods produced in a third country. The threat to the port of Acapulco's commerce from an arbitrary and unpredictable president and his acceptance of the Gadsden treaty resulted in a call for revolt against Santa Anna.

Juan Alvarez, whose autocratic rule centered in the state of Guerrero, led the revolt of the Liberals, now formed into a political movement and an official party, known as the Revolution of Ayutla. His insurrection drew adherents from across the country, including the exiled Liberals from New Orleans anxious to confront the government. Santa Anna took the field, leading an army into Guerrero to destroy Alvarez. In a major battle, the two armies fought to a standstill. Santa Anna, after sending messages announcing a great victory, returned to the capital and, before anyone discovered the results of the fighting, fled to Veracruz and on to exile in Venezuela, not to return until 1876. Santa Anna's departure provided a Liberal political victory, but Conservatives, especially monarchists, remained undefeated and unconvinced.

Liberals on their return to power attempted to revive trade with a new tariff of 30 percent, a sharp reduction of other restrictions, and new ports of entry along the northern border, the Gulf of California, and the Isthmus of Tehuantepec. They issued a new law that extended citizenship with the ownership of real property as an enticement for immigrants. The trickle of immigrants remained quite small until 1876 (numbers are impossible to report because the first national census did not occur until 1895), when the Díaz government brought a new era of political stability that encouraged an increasing number of immigrants— almost 50,000 people joined a nation of 12 million in 1895.[7] The largest number came from the United States, but French, English, and German migrants came as well and were joined by South Americans and Libanese. Chinese immigrants, blocked from entering the United States and British Columbia, came to Mexico and other parts of Pacific Latin America. Nevertheless, changing the economic climate required time.

Liberalism's legitimacy rested on an economic foundation rather than on traditional patriarchal politics and harmony among the social hierarchy. Civil disorder disrupted the republic, sometimes seriously, and drained resources and damaged government prestige. In the case of a Conservative revolt in Puebla in 1856, one of several before the War of the Reform (1858–61), the Liberal government sought a foreign loan of $300,000. Moreover, foreign debt, particularly to European banks, made the threat of forceful debt collection a possibility.

Rapid economic development depended on everything the national government seemingly lacked: tax revenues, investment capital rather than exploitive loans and unserviceable debt, entrepreneurship, technology, and skilled workers. Any hope of rapid progress appeared to require cooperation with foreigners, perhaps even the United States. At the same time, many feared economic cooperation with foreigners would lead Mexico into status as an informal colony or protectorate. Meanwhile, Conservatives continued their campaigns to engineer a national monarchy.

On another front, Liberals gathered as a constituent congress in Querétaro to write a new national constitution. Lawyers, some with experience as governor or other elected offices, made up the majority of delegates. Several, including the recently returned Benito Juárez, had spent time in political exile. Juárez did not have the military experience of many others, and he was notable for his Zapotec heritage, largely hidden by education, social connections, and marriage. Juárez represented the nineteenth-century Liberal commitment to secular and civilian rule.[8]

The delegates began their work on July 4, 1857, a date purposely selected to emphasize the republicanism they hoped to instill. Equality before the law, individual ownership of property, and rigid separation between church and state expressed the tenets of a modern, secular nation. These principles appeared in three degrees named for their authors, the Juárez, Lerdo, and Iglesias laws, that shortly became part of a new constitution of 1857. The congress attempted to create a new citizenry distinguished by confidence in secular political and economic principles. Faith that it could be done by a written document seemed naive, but in the long term the constitution became a milestone toward a secular society.

The convention ended with the signing of the constitution of 1857, a moment in the nation's history as important as the call for independence in 1810. The document restricted church activities in order to promote a secular political and economic regime. Articles fostered landholding by individuals, prohibited corporate ownership of real properties, abolished parallel court systems to create equality before the law, and strove to channel political decision making into voting, by removing the troublesome magnets of political discord: the vice presidency, the privileged positions of military officers, and the influence of Catholic Church leaders. Election under the new constitution elevated Ignacio Comonfort to the presidency and Juárez to chief justice of the Supreme Court, first in the line of succession in case of a presidential vacancy. Comonfort believed, correctly, that the radical liberals, the *puros*, had driven the country to the verge of civil war. Although he signed many radical laws into effect, he waffled in the face of Conservative opposition.

The Conservatives, fully aware of the significance of the constitution of 1857, reacted forcefully. When an attempt to negotiate revisions of the constitution failed, they resorted to rebellion. High Church officials, encouraged by Pope Leo XIII, who had adopted an aggressive policy against Liberalism and unionism across Europe and the Americas, urged sympathetic military officers to rejected the constitution and seize power. Comonfort remained at the head of a coalition unity government. Conservatives dissolved congress, arrested Juárez, and issued their Plan of Tacubaya, which called for a new constitution that restored the powerful position of the church. A national Council of Representatives elected General Félix Zuloaga to assume the presidency in January 1853. Comonfort, before he relinquished office and embarked for exile in New Orleans, ordered Juárez's release. As far as Liberals were concerned, he had abandoned his nation, his office, and his countrymen. Comonfort insisted he was still president, but the Liberal armies supported Juárez, who assumed the presidency of the country in crisis.

President Juárez prudently fled the capital and reestablished a parallel government in Guanajuato. Little could be done except avoid capture. He knew he needed to reach the Liberal stronghold of Veracruz, where he could rely on political support and access to customs revenues and international communications. In April, Juárez embarked from the Pacific coast port of Manzanillo for Veracruz by way of Acapulco, Panama, Havana, and New Orleans. He spent almost a month on board American steamers on the most direct sea route available. With considerable difficulty, the Liberals reestablished their government in the port city of Veracruz and began a protracted civil war.

Meanwhile, President Zuloaga annulled the Lerdo, Juarez, and Iglesias laws and ordered the reinstatement of government employees who had refused to swear allegiance to the constitution of 1857. United States minister John Forsyth Jr. recognized the Zuloaga government, assuming that the Conservatives might be more ready to sell territory. But he soon broke relations with the Conservatives and used recognition as a tool to negotiate with the Liberals. He offered recognition in exchange for selling off parts of northern Mexico. The desperate Liberals indicated that with recognition in hand it might be possible. Both sides played a crafty poker game, with territory and diplomatic recognition as the chips.

Both Liberals and Conservatives borrowed money at ruinous interest rates. The most notorious debt was the Jecker loan. Conservative General Miguel Miramón had obtained 750,000 francs from Jean Baptiste Jecker, a Swiss banker in Mexico, who sold the loan to a French syndicate. Juárez repudiated the loan, but in the meanwhile it provided the Conservatives with minimal operating funds in exchange for 15 million pesos of debt. The Liberals continued to deal with U.S. representatives about possible sale of territory or transit rights. Liberals agreed to a Tehuantepec transit treaty without the provision for troops the U.S. wanted. In 1859, the U.S. Senate refused to ratify what came to be called the McLane-Ocampo Treaty, one of the early plans for Atlantic to Pacific connections, as a result of the belief by northern senators that it somehow favored the South and slavery. Northerners continued to support Juárez.

The War of the Reform evolved into a vicious civil war, punctuated by the atrocities and the senseless destruction characteristic of these kinds of battles. The country appeared to have turned against itself in frustration on both sides. The still substantial church wealth suffered greatly as Liberals seized funds and sold valuables to finance the war efforts. Church leaders made loans to finance Conservative war efforts. No matter what the outcome, in economic terms neither the Catholic Church nor a national government could win. The Liberal generals and the president by succession, Benito Juárez, moved back and forth across the nation during the War of the Reform. Their mobility and their perseverance won out. Finally, on New Year's Day 1861, the Juárez government returned to the capital of the exhausted the nation.

The war engendered endemic violence and banditry in the countryside. Immediately after the war, Juárez responded by recruiting individuals, often former bandits, into a rural constabulary. The Rurales became a symbol of repression from that point on through 1911. Nevertheless, they provided a form of rough justice and order in the countryside.

The war had been won, but not the peace. Conservatives, defiantly backed by the statements of Pope Leo XIII, who ordered excommunication for anyone who accepted the constitution of 1857, turned to Europe for redemption. Conservative leaders refused to concede defeat. Several High Church officials went into exile, where they lobbied at European courts and in the Vatican for troops and financial support to defeat the Liberals. They also tried to identify a prince to replace Juárez.

At its conclusion, the civil war left a staggering foreign debt at high interest rates that the Liberal administration could neither service nor repay on schedule, if ever. Juárez ordered a suspension of debt payments, to give breathing space for the economy to recover. He and the Liberals required that everyone—doing public business in courts, buying or selling real estate, recording births, deaths, and marriages in the public registry, even graduating from the university—swear loyalty to the constitution. In this way, Mexicans had to choose between excommunication and participation in civic society.

Juárez's actions, in particular the suspension of debt payments, provided an opportunity for monarchists to find an ally in the emperor of France to intervene in Mexican affairs.

Napoleon III wanted his empire to exceed that of the first Napoleon and at the same time to reverse the international trend toward republics. He planned to lead a coalition of those European nations that once had been united under Rome (in particular, those that spoke languages derived from Latin: Italy, France, Spain, Portugal, and Romania) and their former colonies in the Western Hemisphere. For the latter, his publicists coined the title Latin America. The notion of being associated with a cultivated Europe as part of a Latin world fell on fertile ground. The term, used to separate the United States culturally from it neighbors, came to be accepted worldwide. Napoleon III hoped to fence off the republican north from Latin America and begin a monarchist revival, perhaps in conjunction with the emperor of Brazil. A monarchist Mexico would symbolically seal the United States north of the Rio Grande to wither in isolation. To isolate the American republic further, he adopted the arguments of Francois Guizot, who warned that the Anglo-Saxon United States verged on destroying the hemisphere's Latin peoples. Napoleon III only needed a pretext to justify intervention to set his plan in motion. The Conservatives offered one. He assumed incorrectly that most Mexicans shared the Conservatives' imperial plans and that his intervention would be welcomed by a grateful Catholic Church and relieved Conservatives in 1861. The French adventure began a year later.

Juárez meanwhile reinstated the Liberal constitution and encouraged the addition of the Epistle of Melchor Ocampo. This letter, written by one of the most prominent Liberals, outlined the rights and responsibilities of men and women in marriage: "The man, whose main sexual attributes are courage and strength, must give and shall always give the woman protection, food and direction. The woman, whose main attributes are self-denial, beauty, compassion, shrewdness and tenderness, must give and shall always give her husband obedience, affability, attention, comfort and advice, treating him with the reverence due to the person who supports and defends us." Incorporated in the civil marriage ceremony, the Ocampo letter served as the legal description of gender relationships and the basis of the family for more than a century.[9]

Juárez's administrative efforts notwithstanding, he presided over a bankrupt government that, by suspending service on foreign debts, provided a convenient pretext for intervention. England, Spain, and France, holding the infamous Jecker loan, wanted to secure customhouse revenues to at least begin repayment. All three agreed to send naval vessels to blockade the port of Veracruz and force collection. France had a hidden agenda. The Liberal assault on the church's role in civil society offered Napoleon III a chance to work on behalf of the pope, with whom he had been at cross-purposes in the struggle over Italian unification. Moreover, he got to play kingmaker and strengthen European alliances by choosing Maximilian, the younger brother of the emperor of the Austro-Hungarian Empire, and his wife, Charlotte, the daughter of the king of Belgium, as the new emperor and empress of Mexico.

A few Spanish and English ships met a full-fledged French invasion force in Veracruz harbor. The English and Spanish commanders, once they grasped the plan, sailed away in protest, and the French officers ordered the invasion of Mexico, with the goal of brushing aside defenders, occupying the country, and placing the new royal couple on the throne. The French made short work of Mexican troops as they advanced toward the capital city, until they arrived just outside of Puebla, called the City of Angels, and known as the most conservative city in the country. The French expected to be greeted there as saviors, who would restore the church and remove the Liberals.

Liberal soldiers, commanded by Texas-born General Ignacio Zaragoza, prayed for rain to bog down the advancing French troops as they prepared for the May 5, 1862, battle. Zaragoza dug his troops in and redoubled his prayers for rain. The French line, overconfident and overly casual, moved forward in single file. Zaragoza and one of his chief officers, Porfirio Díaz, recognized that if the Mexicans could turn the flank (that is, move beyond the end of the French position), they would have the French in the military equivalent of shooting fish in a barrel. Díaz turned the flank and began the slaughter of the stunned French troops. In the brief battle, the French broke and scattered in retreat. The Mexicans pursued but could not complete the destruction of the French army because they became mired in deep mud caused by sudden, heavy rains.

Nevertheless, the Mexican victory over what at the time was regarded as the world's most powerful army stunned politicians and generals across Europe and the Americas. In Mexico, Cinco de Mayo (May 5) became a holiday marking the bravery and daring of national troops. In France, an embarrassed and outraged emperor ordered 5,000 troops, veterans of the Algerian campaigns, to complete the conquest. In Argentina, the national congress named a Buenos Aires street in honor of the Mexican victory. Throughout Europe, leaders began to rethink French leadership and military strength. The Germans, in particular, revised their assessment of the French army.

The French marked time in Veracruz until reinforcements arrived and then renewed their advance to the capital city. Their new respect for the Mexican soldier made them more serious and, therefore, more effective warriors. At the second Battle of Puebla (1863), the French made short work of the defenders, and the Mexican army abandoned not only Puebla but Mexico City as well. The troops and the Juárez government retreated to the north and for next four years survived by constant relocation. The French occupied the capital and arranged for the new rulers to journey from their Mediterranean palace to their new country.

Even before the imperial family arrived, Napoleon III requested a report on Sonora's mineral wealth, as well as an assessment on whether the people in the region could be pacified. He planned that at least a part of northern Mexico could become part of the French Empire, providing a buffer zone with the United States and a monarchist Mexico. Physical control of Mexico depended on French troops, including the Foreign Legion. In sharp contrast, Juárez had independent and therefore unreliable commanders, and indifferently armed and trained soldiers who offered only token resistance before falling back to fight again when the moment seemed more advantageous. As a result the French forces controlled core areas but not the republican fringes.

The glamorous couple Maximilian and Charlotte, known throughout European courts, traveled to Mexico armed with grand ambitions, good intentions, and gilded misinformation provided mostly by high Church informants and conservative Mexican exiles. Ignorance compounded their disregard of troublesome reports about the political situation and the people and set the stage for eventual disaster. Both the emperor and the empress intended to become Mexicans of a sort. Charlotte even hispanized her name to Carlota.

Moreover, they intended to make Mexicans into Europeans. Perhaps, their campaigns in architecture, science, art, and manners would have worked, except that the nation had been invaded and occupied. French, Belgium, and Conservative Mexican troops continued an incessant war to defeat the Liberal troops and local militias loyal to Juárez. Conservative leaders demanded that their new rulers immediately restore church and hacienda properties. These demands the emperor would not meet. Rueful Conservatives gradually became aware that Maximilian shared many of the same secular attitudes of the Liberals.[10]

The war became a test of endurance and money. The nation remained fragmented: the emperor ruled in French-occupied territories but faced constant guerrilla attacks; Juárez ruled close to wherever his black coach stopped, with military commanders and regional strongmen in power in the rest of the nation. At one point, the invaders nearly defeated Juárez and forced him to the border in northern Chihuahua. The president reached the point of preparing to cross the Rio Grande and go into exile if necessary, but his troops held and gradually began to win small but significant battles that forced the imperial allies south.

Napoleon III hoped that the new emperor would be able to organize the nation financially to support most if not all of the cost of war. An annoyed French emperor grumbled that if Maximilian built fewer palaces and theaters and concentrated on bringing honest men into his government, he could curb wasteful spending and allocate sufficient funds to the pacification effort. In 1865 he dispatched a new French financial adviser, Jacques Langlais, reputed to be a talented financial mastermind, to take charge of affairs. This administrative change was too little, too late.

The emperor's army became the victim of American and European events in 1865. In the United States, the Union army defeated the Confederates and won the Civil War. Shortly afterward, the U.S. Secretary of State, William Steward, demanded to know when the French, who were in violation of the U.S. Monroe Doctrine, would leave Mexico (at the same time hinting in the newspapers that a little war in Mexico might be just the thing to reunite the United States). In Europe, Chancellor Otto von Bismarck established the foundations for a stronger Prussia that eventually unified many German-speaking regions and reclaimed territories held by the French. In France, the critics, such as Victor Hugo, who opposed the Mexican adventure doubled and doubled again in response to mounting costs and increasing deaths without victory, honor, or profit for the nation. Napoleon III reconsidered his commitment to Maximilian and Carlota. France turned inward to save itself.

In late 1865, Maximilian received official notification from Napoleon III that the French armies would shortly be recalled because the Liberal armies had been defeated. The French military commander argued that the resistance consisted only of guerrillas and bandits, all of whom he considered to be outlaws not entitled to the rights of soldiers. The commander badgered Maximilian until the latter issued a statement that repeated this conclusion and ordered the penalty of death without trial for these renegades. Ironically, the poorly considered decree subsequently would become the emperor's undoing.

The threat of summary execution made the Liberals fight with greater determination, and they soon received better equipment as well. U.S. Secretary of War Edwin M. Stanton ordered veteran cavalry units and the shipment of surplus arms and ammunition to the region of the Rio Grande. Cavalry officers received orders to protect the war surplus against marauders, Indians, and ex-Confederates, but in the event that Liberal troops crossed the river, the officers and their men were to retreat in good order, leaving the surplus for them. Secretary of State Seward had earlier informed Napoleon III that the U.S. government regarded the French intervention as a violation of the 1823 Monroe Doctrine, which opposed any further European colonization in the Americas.

In this mounting crisis for the imperial regime, the empress Carlota, fearful of the outcome, traveled to Europe with the hope of renewing French support and securing additional military assistance. Napoleon III and his wife refused to receive her and ignored all talk of treaties and promises. Carlota, frantic with foreboding, went to the Vatican in search of the pope's assistance in pressing the French to keep their troops in Mexico. Pope Pius IX received her but refused to intervene because the emperor and empress had not restored church properties. The empress brought with her a draft concordat to regularize Mexican church-state relations, but it failed to sway the pontiff. Carlota collapsed when she received his decision. She recovered physically, but not mentally, and took refuge with her father, the king of Belgium, with whom she lived until 1927, sane only in patches.

News of his wife's collapse and insanity added to Maximilian's sense of impending doom as the French began to depart and Conservative troops faded away. Several advisers urged him and the rest of the court to return to Europe. Maximilian compounded his poor decision to execute Liberal troops as bandits by listening to the counsel of a shadowy character posing as a German priest, Fritz Fischer, who argued that Hapsburg honor and Carlota's sacrifice demanded he remain. The emperor, an avid amateur biologist, went butterfly hunting to ponder the contradictory advice and reach a decision. When he returned, he announced he had decided to fight on.

Following the French withdrawals, two veterans of the War of the Reform, Miguel Miramón and Tomás Mejía, commanded the emperor's army. They held the city of Querétaro against the advancing Liberal troops, with Juárez and his civilian regime in its wake. Fierce fighting enabled the Liberals to surround the city. The two armies dug in for what appeared to be a long siege.

Maximilian, with his new resolve, decided to march his bodyguard with additional reinforcements to take command of his army at Querétaro. This relief column managed to fight its way into the city, but the Liberals slammed the door behind it and restored the siege. Weeks dragged on, with both soldiers and civilians beginning to suffer from food shortages, limited water, and edgy nerves. The emperor ordered one unit to fight its way out and go to the capital for ammunition, supplies, and reinforcements to break the siege. Maximilian wanted to show that he could carry on as normal; his bravado included ordering wine and sheet music with the bullets and food. Many observers saw this as proof he had lost touch with reality. It mattered little, because the commander and his troops, after escaping the city and reaching the capital, made no effort to return.

The Liberals broke the siege in June 1867 when they brokered an agreement with some Conservative troops who were allowed to escape in exchange for letting the Liberals through their lines into the city. The Liberals surprised the Conservative high command, including the emperor, and quickly placed them under arrest and awaited the arrival of Juárez. The successful occupation of Querétaro inspired Porfirio Díaz and others to storm the capital city and, with difficult fighting, to capture it. These two victories ended the French occupation and empire in Mexico.

There remained the question of the emperor and his two commanders, Mejía and Miramón. In Querétaro, a circus of conspirators, including the mistress of self-promotion and onetime trapeze artist Princess Salm-Salm, tried to arrange Maximilian's escape. Across Mexico, voices demanded retribution, and others urged generosity. From Europe and the United States, national leaders such as President Andrew Johnson and celebrities such as Victor Hugo pled for the emperor's life. President Benito Juárez ordered trials for treason for the generals and murder for the emperor for ordering the execution of Liberal troops. Once the guilty verdicts had been returned, Juárez announced there would be no clemency. A firing squad escorted the three to the top of the Hill of the Bells on June 19, 1867, where Maximilian offered the place of honor in the center to Miramón (despite the paintings by Édouard Manet) and gave each of the riflemen a gold coin not to shoot them in the face. The squad executed the three.

Tributes to Maximilian in music, poetry, literature, and painting swept across Europe, attempting to excuse him as a well-intentioned, misguided nobleman. Mexicans expressed some sympathy for him, although mixed with amazement at his ignorance of their country. Juárez remained unmoved by imperial pretensions, no matter how utopian, based on military conquest.

Juárez made it evident immediately that he intended to restore civilian rule to the nation. He thanked his commanding officers but indicated that his government's gratitude did not extend beyond a heart-felt thank-you without political and financial rewards. In a reorganization of the military, he soon slashed the size of the army and its officer corps by half. His guiding principles came from the constitution of 1857, and his associates he chose from the extreme Liberals who had surrounded him during exile in New Orleans, the War of the Reform, and the French intervention.

As he worked at restoring republican government, he attempted to erase many imperial attributes, but some he could not and others he chose not to destroy. Maximilian had attempted urban renewal following the Paris model, carving out a new ceremonial avenue named for his

The execution of Maximilian of the Hapsburg family, the French-imposed emperor of Mexico, on June 19, 1867, shocked Europeans as an example of what they believed was Mexican barbarism. The artist Édouard Manet painted several canvases of the execution that contain historical errors. The emperor, shot to death with his leading generals, Miguel Miramón and Tomás Mejía, did not occupy the center place of honor (he gave the spot to Miramón), nor did he wear the sombrero that Manet placed on his head. Erich Lessing/ Art Resource, NY

wife, which went from the center of town to Chapultepec palace, his refurbished royal residence. Juárez renamed the avenue "La Reforma," and, after stripping the palace of many of its imperial trappings and having them sold at auction, he reappointed Chapultepec as the presidential residence.

Of more consequence, Juárez, the *benemérito* (meritorious individual) of his country, understood that the imperial interlude had weakened and discredited conservatism, now linked to foreign intervention. He recognized also that an exhausted liberalism had triumphed, but at a cost he did not want to repeat even to a slight degree. Economic and political stability, the goal of both sides, offered the possibility of unifying the country and proceeding toward the developmental goals laid out earlier by Miguel Lerdo. Release of Conservative prisoners and an offer of conciliation toward those who had collaborated with the French made the point that the executions for treason would not be widespread. Those who died in front of a firing squad on the Hill of Bells appeared to be enough.

In 1868, Juárez, after serving as president for a decade, faced election for the first time. He had assumed the office by succession when Comonfort had fled Mexico and, because of the incessant civil and foreign wars, continued in the position when elections had been postponed. A proclamation calling for national election also contained a referendum in which the president made suggestions to modify the constitution of 1857 to soften its unyielding liberalism. He proposed to allow the clergy to vote, ended residency requirements for federal deputies, proposed the creation of a senate, increased presidential power, and offered a new succession arrangement. If the referendum passed, each of states would need to modify their constitutions accordingly.

Not surprisingly, Juárez's move to the right appealed to Conservatives but not to hard-core Liberals, although its defenders noted that many of the suggested changes mirrored those of the constitution of 1824. Municipalities feared that a more conservative Juárez jeopardized local autonomy. As a consequence, the referendum set off small, local revolts in a handful of states, ironically reinforcing the notion that the country needed more central government control. Under mounting Liberal pressure, Juárez withdrew the referendum, but he arranged for the enactment of some changes through legislation.

Juárez easily won the presidency. The time had come to rebuild the economy and to revive development programs, such as the railroad from Veracruz to Mexico City initiated during the last Santa Anna regime, that had been thrown off track by civil war and foreign intervention. These activities occupied his four-year term of office.

As the end of his presidential term approached, it became clear that after years of battling for survival, Juárez believed that he had become indispensable. He decided to run again. Many felt his fourteen years in office had resulted in increasingly autocratic behavior and now bordered on dictatorial authority. Justification for an authoritarian regime could be found in the new European philosophy of Auguste Comte. Comtian positivism linked order and progress with the goal of a scientific, rather than political, government. It drew on the authoritarianism inherent in the eighteenth-century Enlightenment's notion of human perfection. It also posited an evolutionary development over three stages of history ending in the final technocratic regime under a benevolent director.

Pedro Contreras Elizalde, considered the first Mexican positivist, had studied medicine in France, knew Comte, and became a charter member of the Société Positiviste in 1848. He married one of Juárez's daughters when he returned home and served in the government. Gabino Barreda, the educator responsible for the spread of Comte's philosophy, also studied medicine in Paris, attended Comte's lectures, and knew Elizalde. Barreda organized the National Preparatory School that opened with a class of ninety students in 1868. An important generation of the national elite passed through the school, including José Yves Limantour, the powerful secretary of the treasury during the Díaz regime.

Barreda's other contribution, perhaps equally important, involved a psychological recasting of national history to give value to a traumatic past. Employing Comte's notion of stages, he portrayed the nation's history as an epic struggle between darkness and enlightenment and suggested another era had just begun. The valiant battle against the French ended with a victory for all humanity, one that saved the republican ideal from a monarchist resurgence. Barreda's historical analysis made it all seem worthwhile, in spite of the suffering.

Former U.S. secretary of state Seward, invited by President Juárez to visit Mexico, echoed this interpretation as he placed the U.S. Civil War and the French intervention in the center of the epic struggle against archaic monarchies. He predicted that both republics would now be free to demonstrate the material advantages of republicanism. Juárez, the principal hero of the struggle, stood as the benevolent ruler that Comte favored.

Nevertheless, two plausible candidates opposed Juárez's reelection: Sebastian Lerdo de Tejada, the brother of Miguel, represented middle-of-the-road civilian Liberalism; General Porfirio Díaz presented himself as the candidate of veterans, especially officers, who felt their service had been ignored when Juárez cut the army by some 16,000 troops. In a disputed election, Juárez again won. Lerdo de Tejada joined the government, but Díaz announced a revolt to overturn the government from his Oaxacan hacienda, La Noria. This revolt tested public sentiment for a coup d'état, and, finding little support, Díaz ended the effort and waited.

The complex political situation became more complicated after just a few months, when Juárez died. A new election gave the presidency to Sebastian Lerdo de Tejada, who manipulated the counting of the votes in his favor. Díaz and the political elite accepted the results. It became obvious that President Lerdo de Tejada preferred a strong centralized government and a captive, obedient congress responsive to his wishes. Opponents claimed that he acted like a czar.

Under President Lerdo de Tejada the reforms earlier suggested by Juárez became law, including the creation of a senate. Laws against wearing clerical robes in public and further restriction on religious displays reinvigorated Liberal anticlericalism, while annoying church leaders. As for economic policies, President Lerdo de Tejada remained committed to Juárez's insistence on civilian rule and economic development, especially railroad building. The latter did not include extending rails north to the United States because, as he explained it, "between strength and weakness, a desert should remain." By 1876, the country had only 416 miles of track, but with plans for a more extensive network. Nevertheless, the years of peace helped a general economic recovery, noticeable in mining.

The 1876 elections matched the incumbent president, Lerdo de Tejada, against the persistent general, Porfirio Díaz. The general campaigned and made promises that addressed a wide range of complaints from the northern borderlands, a region crucial for arms shipment if necessary, to disgruntled federalists upset with the centralism of Lerdo de Tejada. These elements could be expected to rise up in revolt if the election did not go as hoped. When the election results indicated another term for the current president, Díaz issued his Plan of Tuxtepec, which demanded effective suffrage and no reelection—that is, honest vote counting and a one-term presidency .

This time the country rallied to Porfirio Díaz. Joined by other army veterans and disenchanted Liberals, Diaz plotted revolution from Texas. Then he left Brownsville to return by ship to Tampico. Suspicious authorities halted and searched the vessel but failed to discover the well-concealed Díaz. A crew member later told the general that they protected him because one of the sailors had noticed his Masonic ring, and the ship's crew included several lodge members. Díaz landed safely and took command of the revolt.

The Revolution of Tuxtepec soon swept to its victorious conclusion. After a few battles and much political posturing, the Porfirians held supervised elections and, as expected, announced Díaz's election. Meanwhile, a beleaguered Lerdo de Tejada fled to the United States. Few sensed that a major turning point in national history had been reached. Diaz ushered in a prolonged period of rapid agricultural commercialization, industrialization, and unbalanced social progress.[11]

Many Liberal achievements occurred with Juárez's regime after the French intervention. Reinvigorated and instilled with confidence by the victory against the French and the intellectual amalgamation of positivism, Liberals felt confirmed in their beliefs. Juárez's movement away from the extremes of the old *puros* appealed to chastened Conservatives. Many of the latter concluded that they could accept a moderate form of liberalism and that national unity required conceding to liberalism's dominance. The legal changes brought both sides together politically. The nation began to show signs of prosperity that could be attributed, rightly or not, to the impact of new ideas and shared ideology. While some of the goals of liberalism were realized, the school of thought retained its harshness toward the lower classes, including Indians, based on their resistance to modern values and methods. But Liberals had successfully overcome the years of wartime invasion, defeat, and occupation to lay the constitutional and legal frameworks for political stability and economic development. General Porfirio Díaz led forward a group of army veterans who inherited the nation they had first defended against both the United States and France and then helped build under the Liberals and Benito Juárez.

CHAPTER FIVE

Progress for Mexico and Some Mexicans, 1876–1911

Porfirio Díaz, born in 1830 in Oaxaca, shared his native state with Benito Juárez, born a generation earlier in 1806. Díaz's expectations differed from Juárez's, as did his reactions and experiences during the war with the United States and the French intervention in which both men played important roles. President Juárez became an icon cherished by Liberals, admired for his ability to survive and for his perseverance in prevailing over his enemies. His death in 1872 at age sixty-six opened political competition and inspired new efforts to fulfill liberalism's promise. General Díaz seized national power four years after the death of Juárez. At age forty-six, Díaz was at the height of physical energy and, with an unsurpassed military record, had widespread support among Liberal veterans.[1]

General Diaz's commitment to the nation could not be questioned—he possessed impeccable Liberal credentials. He personified for many the victorious Liberal struggle to preserve the nation. He had fought in the victory over the French in the May 5, 1862, battle for Puebla. Later captured by the French, he escaped to continue the fight against the forces of Maximilian and entered Mexico City as the conquering general, making possible the return of Juárez's government to the capital. His revolt against the president was excused as frustration with Juárez in decline. He understood the importance of image and gravitas, so that he gave expression to his patriotism in personal gestures. He registered his daughter, Luz Aurora Victoria Díaz, on May 5, 1875, so her birthday fell on the anniversary of the Cinco de Mayo victory over the French. He also held his own birthday celebrations on the anniversary of Hidalgo's call for independence. He projected stability and faith in progress with firmness and conviction in the nation. When necessary he appeared in military uniform, but more often he dressed in civilian clothing with a Masonic emblem. Díaz appeared to be a stalwart officer, preserving the flame of Liberalism, and leading a generation of veterans working to propel the nation into the modern era.

The new president set out to expand his national constituency to mirror his position as chief of the nation. He built his regime on the camaraderie of soldiers with Liberal convictions. He turned to veterans, who had fought in the war of the French intervention, because he believed that patriotic men could be trusted. Believing these men who had struggled for the nation deserved tangible recognition for their service, he rewarded them as Juárez had not. With a soldier's respect for other soldiers, he planned to redeem those who had fought during the U.S. intervention and the War of the Reform but then chose the wrong side during the French intervention. He understood officers—their commitment to the nation, their loyalty to fellow soldiers, and their obedience to command. With men such as these, Díaz believed he could preserve national honor, achieve progress, and claim international esteem.

Díaz, during his first presidencies (1876–80, 1884–88, and 1888–92), focused on creating national unity to legitimate his seizure of power, secure his government, and legislate the enabling laws for the constitution of 1857. Mobilizing veterans and forging cooperation among the different state and national leaders required delicate juggling of his commitment to redeem opponents with forgiveness and prompt attention to challenges to his authority. He displayed the talents of command, persuasion, and compromise at the same time that he rewarded loyalty and punished opponents.

The president relied on a Pan or Palo (carrot-and-stick) policy. For those who supported him, he provided political and economic opportunities. Those who challenged him faced exile or death. Rural revolts tested his policies. In reaction to the seizure of land by railway speculators and other claimants using the Lerdo Law, uprisings occurred in twelve states, including Mexico, Puebla, Querétaro, and others, and reached the northern border. Francisco Zalacosta and other agrarian leaders formed the Gran Comité Communero that issued the Ley del Pueblo (1879). Their proclamation called for the distribution of land to landless families and smallholders with property valued at less than 3,000 pesos to be paid for over a period of years. Municipal authorities were to provide low-interest loans for seed, machinery, and other agricultural needs, financed by special agrarian banks located in every state. These and similar proposals surfaced again and again during the Porfirian era. Zalacosta, with a few hundred men, sacked and burned haciendas across several states for more than a year and a half. Federal troops eventually defeated them and executed the survivors. The ruthless suppression of opponents marked Díaz's political policies throughout his regime.

In addition to using the stick, Porfirio made state and national political appointments carrots for his supporters. He also created opportunities to lure individuals to invest in new enterprises, especially exporting minerals and commercial crops, with tax exemptions and access to financing. In his economic plans, he sought to renew foreign investment. This required deft management of contractual arrangements because the French had used debt collection to justify intervention, and because the United States verged on replacing Great Britain as the dominant economic power in the Americas. The United States had improved its position in Mexico by supporting the Juárez regime. With the Liberal victory in 1867, Juárez had broken diplomatic relations with every nation that had recognized the Maximilian regime and canceled all treaties in existence with those nations prior to the French intervention. The break with France, England, and other European nations enabled the United States to gain a clear commercial advantage.

Díaz's carrot-and-stick policy enabled the regime to survive its entire term—something that had happened only twice before during the fifty-five years since independence. Part of his success resulted from the question of presidential succession. In a message to Congress in 1877, Díaz pledged to honor the no-reelection statement that he made during his successful rebellion to seized power. He submitted a constitutional amendment that prohibited any incumbent president from being elected for the succeeding presidential term or occupying the presidency until four years had passed. With congressional approval, Díaz promulgated the amendment on his favorite day, May 5, the date of the victory over the French. He announced that he anticipated that state legislators would choose to apply the same restrictions to governors.

Díaz remained popular as his term ended, particularly among those who believed that stability could best be assured by a military officer, but he kept his pledge to step down. A half dozen candidates with presidential aspirations entered the race; of them, Justo Benítez and General Manuel González stood out. Benítez, another native of Oaxaca, had served as Díaz's civilian private secretary during the French intervention; since then, he had become an important congressional leader. Despite their close wartime association, Díaz did not support him because he lacked military experience and had an independent power base in Congress.

Rather, Díaz arranged for his fellow general Manuel González to become president. González had all the right qualifications, except for the mistake of having fought on the conservative side during the War of the Reform. Nevertheless, his candidacy appealed to both reconciled

Conservatives and Liberal veterans. Díaz stressed that the two men had long-standing ties. Their friendship rested on the battlefield camaraderie of soldiers who together had faced the enemy. González served some time as Diaz's chief of staff during the struggle against the French, supported his former commander in the aborted La Noria revolt, and joined the Revolution of Tuxtepec. Elected governor of Michoacán, he took a leave of absence when Díaz offered him the cabinet position of secretary of war.

González won the presidential office.[2] The formal election results announced in the Chamber of Deputies gave González 11,528 votes and the runner-up, Benítez, only 1,368, with a few hundred votes for additional candidates. The total of 15,026 votes cast indicated the small size of the electorate. Minor disturbances orchestrated by defeated candidates caused fears of an armed uprising, but they quickly faded. The comparatively smooth electoral process encouraged newspaper editors to trumpet the election results as proof the nation had moved into a new era of stable politics.

Manuel González, despite his close association with Díaz, had ambitions of his own. His programs put into practice provisions of the Liberal constitution and shaped government polices for more than a decade. Resolute continuation of the campaign for political order required his attention. Then he turned to the creation of a framework favorable to economic growth. He, his cabinet, and Liberal congressmen pushed to implement the economic provisions of the constitution of 1857 through the enactment of new mining, land, and surveying laws. This enabling legislation encouraged individual, private enterprises in silver mining, commercial agricultural, telegraphic communications, and railroad construction financed with foreign capital. The mining law removed the Spanish colonial tradition that gave the government ownership of the subsoil and water rights; the land law assaulted communal landownership; and the surveying law prompted the survey of the national territory to provide information for government planning and individual industry. He signed new contracts for national telegraphic communications and rail systems with ties to the U.S. market.

Mining, the economic engine of the colony, once again became the most important sector, but it broadened beyond silver in response to the new federal mining law. The law's most significant change allowed private titles that could serve as collateral for loans. The proviso required that the mine be continuously worked for at least twenty-six weeks each year by at least six miners. Instead of the older horde of small nuisance taxes on the industry, companies paid one tax shared by federal and state governments based on the value of ores. The law theoretically created safety standards in the mines, but it contained no enforcement procedures. Mining companies benefited from other laws that provided coal, iron, and mercury (used in the silver refining process) with an exemption from all taxes for fifty years. The laws encouraged large-scale operations using advanced technology that made it possible to mine low-grade deposits. U.S. investment in mining, under the new laws, grew from $3 million in 1884 to $55 million in 1892.

The land and surveying laws of 1883 sought to encourage occupation and productive use of unoccupied lands—that is, unsurveyed lands without individual owners. The law put holdings of communal groups and territories of nomadic peoples at risk because it placed the proof of ownership on the landholder. Small and communal holders found it difficult, often impossible, to produce titles. Between 1881 and 1889 companies surveyed some 32 million hectares of theoretically unoccupied land and received 27.5 million hectares in compensation, equivalent to 14 percent of the nation's surface area. The law set the stage for large-scale commercial agricultural operations as irrigation and machinery began to dominate economic activity, especially in the north.

Economic expansion required long-term credit, and banking lagged behind with only two institutions that served the republic. The British established the Bank of London and Mexico in 1864 to facilitate business, and the government had created the Monte de Piedad, the National Pawnshop that allowed the poor to raise capital on their merger possessions, received deposits, discounted and collected bills, and issued bank notes. A handful of state governments chartered banks that served a small number of clients. In addition, local moneylenders extended loans, advanced wages, and gave short-term credit for weddings and other such social expenditures. The church placed limited funds in trusted private hands that financed some property mortgages. The inefficient and inadequate system barely functioned. Paper money circulated at a discount and could not be easily regulated.

Responding to this financial situation, González worked through Congress to legislate the new commercial code of 1884 and laid the groundwork for an efficient modern banking system. At the president's urging, bankers created the Banco National de Mexico that provided the government a line of credit to a maximum of 8 million pesos, became the depository of public funds, and, with a monopoly on emissions, circulated the only notes recognized as legal tender. Bank assets jumped from approximately 3 million pesos to 30 million by the end González's term. In tandem with creation of a central bank, the

Ministry of Development during the administration functioned with a budget larger than that of the Ministry of War. In González's final year in office, the development agency absorbed a third of the federal budget.

President González and his diplomats faced a number of vexing relationships that made the search for foreign investments complicated. Diplomacy with the United States focused on tariffs, an outdated commercial agreement, Indian raiders using the border for protection, incursions by U.S. troops in pursuit of marauders, smuggling both ways across the frontier, and disputed islands in the Rio Grande. Dealings with the British centered on debts and recognition after eighteen years of suspended interest payments and broken relations. On the southern border, Guatemalans claimed that Mexico had illegally occupied Chiapas and the province of Soconusco. Guatemalan diplomats astutely tried to lure the U.S. government to provide arbitrators for the dispute, much to the annoyance of Mexican officials. Moreover, as in the north, the southern boundary remained effectively unmarked.

In every direction, President González and his advisers looked at dangerous issues that awaited resolution. They solved many of them and, except for one, moved the rest toward reasonable settlement. His one major failure involved tariffs and rationalization of trade agreements.

Other difficulties notwithstanding, González addressed the restructuring of the international debt to improve diplomatic relations generally, and to encourage further foreign investment. Díaz, during his first term, had taken almost a year to secure Washington's recognition. Payment of financial obligations created a favorable financial climate that laid the groundwork for subsequent U.S. investments. As early as 1880, Mexico turned to the United States for more than 50 percent of its imports and for direct foreign investment and loans relied on Wall Street bankers (with significant indirect British, European, and Canadian participation).

Proximity and diplomatic ties shifted the economic focus from London and Paris to New York and Washington. Nevertheless, the González administration worked to reestablish diplomatic relations with European governments by refinancing and resuming payment of European debts. Cabinet minister Matías Romero took the first tentative steps to restructure the loans and renewed relationships, beginning with France in 1880. Great Britain, by far the largest holder of Mexican debts, remained without formal diplomatic ties until 1885. The final steps in the debt process did not come until Díaz returned to office in

1884 and appointed fellow Oaxacan Manuel Dublán as secretary of the treasury. Over the next four years, Dublán consolidated the entire foreign debt in what was called the 1888 Dublán Convention, regarded as a masterpiece of fiscal management, with bonds valued at 10.5 million British pounds bearing 6 percent interest. Germans purchased a majority of the new bonds and made it possible for the Mexican government to borrow new money at reasonable rates.

Economic and diplomatic relations affected the troubling issue of rail connections with U.S. lines. Many individuals, inside and outside the government, feared that a railroad connection would allow U.S. expansionists to ride the rails in a manner similar to their conquest of the western United States. As a result, congressmen had voted against the construction of a new line from Nuevo Laredo, across the Rio Grande from Laredo, Texas, to Mexico City, but President González pressured them to approve the route. As a result, his administration initiated major railway construction, supported by subsidies that totaled more than a million pesos for the two lines that connected Mexico City to the United States. Taxes imposed on railroads and their traffic offset much of the subsidies but did not result in surplus funds. Tracks surged during his term from 1,000 kilometers in 1880 to 6,000 in 1884.

The administration also put in place rules regulating railroads that required advanced government approval of construction plans, creation of safety practices, publication of set schedules, and required that all employees in contact with the public speak Spanish. The law of 1881 placed government representatives on corporate boards to ensure attention to these regulations. Besides stimulating commerce, the extension of lines into isolated areas strengthened federal control. Using the Mexican Central and the Mexican National, Mexicans shipped 70 percent of their exports in the early 1890s to the United States.

The rails provided a honeymoon opportunity for Díaz, who had remarried in 1883. He took his wife, Carmen Romero Rubio, as the end of González's term approached, to the United States. The holiday offered the opportunity for meetings with businessmen and politicians in preparation for shaping Mexican-U.S. relationships when Díaz returned to office. As the private cars of the honeymoon party traveled across the eastern United States, each evening featured a dinner with state and city authorities with the new bride acting as the hostess. In New York, she attempted to visit her godfather, Sebastian Lerdo de Tejada, driven by her husband from the presidency into exile in 1876, with the hope of reconciling with him. The former president refused to receive her and refused as well to return from exile.

In other regards, the honeymoon proved to be a successful diplomatic campaign. Moreover, it set a pattern for the activities of Carmen, when she returned to Mexico and became the First Lady. She took full advantage of her family's social position to establish networks for Díaz with social, economic, and religious elites. Her role as hostess provided the gruff general president opportunities for informal interaction with leaders, such as Archbishop Antonio de Labastida y Dávalos of Mexico City, that would have been extremely difficult to arrange otherwise. Carmen's social events increased cooperation by the elites, regardless of Liberal or Conservative affiliation.

Meanwhile, Díaz's subordinates made certain that González entertained no thought of remaining or returning to the presidency by promoting charges of fiscal misconduct against him that dragged on until 1888. In addition, they publicized his adulterous behavior and, worse, his civil divorce, which scandalized upper-class society. Public and personal attacks aside, González and his administration laid the groundwork for the next twenty-five years with economic programs. His presidency, like a hinge, swung Mexico toward successful economic development for the rest of the century.

Díaz easily won reelection in 1884 and quickly moved to emphasize three major projects regarding public order, church-government relations, and financial development that built on González's foundation. His campaigns aimed to establish widespread civil order by eliminating local agrarian violence, ubiquitous banditry, and political upheaval; to conclude the long-standing struggle between civil government and church authorities with what he regarded as an appropriate reconciliation; to foster economic development by increasing the export of silver, sugar, and possibly coffee and rubber; and to expand the rail and telegram lines by attracting foreign investors.

In his domestic campaign for social and political stability, he took care to balance both individuals and institutions as a technique to preempt opposition. The old general continued to recognize and reward veterans, but he carefully balanced the generals as individuals and as a group. He had begun restructuring the army almost immediately after his seizure of power in 1876; González had continued to implement changes during his administration, and Díaz, when he returned to office in 1884, completed the process. He intended to create apolitical, professional officers with a new organizational plan that divided the republic into zones that covered several states commanded by a general, and divided those into *jefaturas de armas*, district commands that provided military presence in a state, a territory, or a single city, especially ports.[3] In particularly sensitive areas, he created commandancies, outside the chain of command, that took orders directly from the minister of war.

The number of such divisions depended on the president, as did the size of the force. The absence of a centralized facility for enlisted men meant that each commander trained his own soldiers. Shifting officers around the republic limited the danger of a commander forging close connections with his men, perhaps then turning them into political followers. A sudden reassignment or change in designation could leave a politically ambitious officer isolated. The reorganization plan made it difficult for any officer to organize a military challenge to the regime, while maintaining sufficient strength to deal with emergencies.

Equally as important, the new structure left intact the system that rewarded loyalty. In the absence of an army supply system and effective fiscal accounting, the government allocated funds based on the number of men on unit rosters. Inflating numbers and skimming payrolls provided a bonus for commanders at all levels. Corruption often made officers too comfortable to contemplate revolt. Díaz did not trouble himself with the financial lives of the officer corps. Nor did he worry much about the quality of recruits. States assigned to supply quotas turned to impressments that swept up individuals that communities sought to rid themselves of for various reasons. Local troublemakers, minor criminals, and political or personal opponents of local authorities suffered impressment. Díaz eliminated the Second Reserve, the local and state militias, leaving state governors without independent military forces. The president claimed that his reorganization provided flexibility in case of security needs. It also fragmented the chain of command. Reluctant soldiers and contented officers had advantages for the president.

The army as institution soon found its duties circumscribed. Defense of the nation against foreign invasion served as its primary justification, but relying on the army for everyday law enforcement suggested that the country had not been pacified. Such an interpretation might frighten away investors, so Díaz turned to the notorious rural constabulary (the Rurales), expanded its numbers, duties, and visibility, and changed its image.[4] Fashionable *charro* uniforms modeled after the dress of early nineteenth-century bandits, the *platereos* who studded their clothes and saddles with silver, gave them visibility, like the red uniforms of the Royal Canadian Mounted Police. Dressed in light gray bolero jackets, tight-fitting suede leather trousers braided and decorated with silver, and gray heavy felt sombreros, they paraded in civil celebrations in towns and cities and, deployed in rural regions, especially the areas of the most economic development, guaranteed peace and order in the countryside.

The Rurales attended to their duty with ruthless efficiency, eliminating banditry and armed agrarian and political challenges to the regime. They rarely brought bandits or insurgents to trial. Prisoners generally fell victim to an administrative order that encouraged the Rurales to shoot anyone who attempted to escape. The law of flight (*ley de fuga*) led to the Rurales' reputation for extralegal enforcement practices. Often their presence alone secured the peace. They quickly became the symbols of an orderly nation. Foreigners delighted in repeating the old saw that anyone could carry a gold bar from one end of Mexico to the other in perfect safety.

The president, who treasured order above judicial niceties, honored the Rurales each year at the capital's finest restaurant, the Elysian Tivoli with its fashionable casino and lovely gardens. At noon, he reviewed the mounted constabulary from the restaurant's balcony and then received their representatives for an elegant dinner that included a guest list of prominent and wealthy Mexicans and foreigners arranged around a horseshoe-shaped table. At the end of the evening, the guests joined their host in a champagne toast to the corps of Rurales.

Diners, at the ceremonial dinner or on other occasions, as they stepped out of the Elysian Tivoli likely encountered the city's recently created police. Some 3,000 strong, dressed in blue uniforms topped with Parisian-style kepis, almost indistinguishable from the French Gendarmerie, they made sure that only acceptable people entered the best parts of town, thus creating a facade of safety and modernity. They patrolled the parks and gardens scattered through the fashionable sections of the capital to maintain their peaceful elegance. Both the Rurales and the city police took over the general campaign of ensuring social tranquillity. They balanced the army, which still had responsibilities for the campaigns against indigenous peoples in both the north and south of the nation and, occasionally, for suppressing unionization efforts and strikes among miners and factory workers.

Crushing any challenge to the regime included ensuring local compliance with presidential policies. Díaz used the need to complete domestic political reforms to justify a constitutional change that allowed for his reelection. He understood the importance of state politicians, particularly governors, in assuring regional peace. Governors presented the president's policies to his citizens and represented the state's interests to the president. A governor's success rested on his relationship with Díaz. In politics, the governor might suggest candidates to represent the state in the federal congress, recommending individuals who were compliant with his projects.

The president also instituted appointed regional prefects. Each of these officials, called the *jefe politico*, was responsible to the federal government for ensuring implementation of his programs. The *jefe politico* had responsibility for maintaining order and the proper functioning of the municipality. The prefecture went against the tradition of sovereign municipal governments, the *municipio libre*, as the jefes exercised authority over local land and taxes, suppressed local militias, and could call on the Rurales or the military for assistance.

The army, the Rurales, the city police, and regional prefects created the orderly day-to-day life that allowed the regime to undertake social programs. The Porfirian generation, with its European intellectual, fashion, and cultural orientation, sought to mold society to fit its perception of the nation. Municipal leaders, especially in Mexico City, used new laws to redefine poverty, unemployment, and homelessness—that is, the daily life lived in the streets—as begging, vagrancy, loitering, prostitution, and drunkenness. Municipal authorities attempted to clear the streets of mendicants, vendors, Indians, and rural people in general. The search for the appropriate urban appearance led to clothing ordinances that required European-style trousers and dresses rather than the rural pajamas and indigenous *huipiles*, and, at least in Guadalajara and Colima, levied fines on the large brims of rural sombreros. Dress codes reached to occupations, requiring special hats or clothing and licenses for hack drivers, newspaper vendors, and porters, among others. Those that resisted these laws encountered the new urban police, who were eager to enforce modernity.

City and national government officials promoted the appearance of the progressive nation at every opportunity. They published guides in English, French, and Spanish, with lavish illustrations that described opportunities to tempt the most cautious investors. They distributed the promotional volumes to businessmen's libraries from New York to Kansas City, London to Birmingham, and Paris to Marseilles.

Foreign expositions provided another opportunity for concrete demonstrations of progress. The federal, state, and local governments sent extensive exhibits to the fairs in Paris, Berlin, Chicago, St. Louis, New Orleans, and other cities worldwide. A working model of the proposed Tehuantepec Ship-Railway delighted visitors to the Cotton Exposition in New Orleans in 1884, and the military band so captivated listeners that it was invited to the presidential inauguration in

Washington, D.C. The 1889 Paris Exposition awarded Mexican exhibitors twenty-five grand prizes and a host of lesser awards. Again at world fairs in Chicago, Buffalo, and St. Louis, Mexican exhibits impressed audiences. Diaz's efforts assured his countrymen and foreigners, especially potential investors, that the nation had achieved stability and welcomed development projects.

Other progressive nations of the era shared secular government as a defining characteristic. The Liberals had won victories against the church and its Conservative supporters during the bitter midcentury wars that ended in 1867. The Liberals had institutionalized a new secular nation in the constitution of 1857. Later, the 1871 Penal Code addressed family and domestic issues, building on the marriage statements including the Epistle of Melchor Ocampo that formerly the church had supervised. Even so, social life remained cloaked in the popular versions of Catholic beliefs. During the 1880s, Díaz took steps toward reconciliation with the church as part of his general program of ending divisions within the national elites. The president had no intention of changing the secular nature of politics, but he sought to have church support for his social programs and approval for his political regime.

Díaz's first major effort followed his marriage to Carmen. Archbishop Antonio Labastida y Dávalos of Mexico City officiated at the wedding and continued to visit her home to hear confession. Díaz began having polite conversations with the archbishop following the weekly visits, and they soon reached a working agreement on church-government relations. Díaz kept the anticlerical laws in place, but he did not enforce them. In exchange, the clerics gave up their conspiracies against the Liberal government and became supporters of the Porfirian regime. The president retained the legal authority to crack down if the church leaders acted against him. The accommodation with church officials shifted the focus of Liberal politics away from anticlerical issues campaigns against both Catholic and Protestant groups.

Although Protestant congregations had small numbers of adherents, by 1892 some 385 churches functioned throughout the republic. Members of the president's cabinet even helped promote such institutions as the YMCA. On Carmen's saint day, July 16, the couple celebrated the working alliance with the archbishop. Díaz as the spokesman of the Liberals and a practicing Mason did not attend church services, but at the end of the ceremony for the Virgin of Carmen, he regularly joined his wife to receive a group of the poor and humble.

During the years from 1892 to 1911, the Porfirian system achieved dramatic successes as its policies matured. Diaz had returned to the presidency in 1884, and, following the constitutional amendment, continued to win every four-year term through the election of 1910. The secure political situation resulted from the well-policed society, the accommodation with the church, and the development of the economy.

The greatest social change came as memories of war and violence faded. The veterans and survivors of the Liberal wars and French intervention died. Only Díaz himself aged gracefully. An assertive, ambitious, better-educated generation from the capital city took their places. The new generation changed both faces and attitudes. Those who began taking charge in the 1890s lacked experience outside of the classroom and foreign travel, but their eagerness for achievement led to zealous impatience and ruthless indifference toward the past and tactless frustration with obstacles and opponents in the present.

In the places of his former military colleagues, Díaz turned to these young men from the capital city who had earned college degrees, especially in technical and financial disciplines. As a result, his regime increasingly became a technocratic administration. These technocrats followed the general views of positivism, especially its slogan: "Order and Progress," promoted by a loosely organized group formed during the presidency of Manuel González. Members included the minister of finance José Limantour, Diaz's father-in-law Manuel Romero Rubio, and the minister of education Justo Sierra. Their views predominated in the national preparatory school and the national university and shaped the education of the new generation.

These positivists believed in a secular republic with strong administrative leadership, liberal politics, capitalist economics, and rational social programs. Their confidence in science provided an article of faith. One newspaper writer coined the term Cientificos (scientists) to poke fun at them, and the label stuck. These technocrats pushed forward the presidential programs, so that the economy boomed with expanding railroads, mineral and agricultural exports, and developing textile, cigarette, and food-processing industries. The reputation of the nation reached the heights predicted by Alexander von Humboldt and other writers at the time of independence.

International attention focused on the regime became more intense in response to promotional literature as political guests and potential investors visited the country, motivated by the displays at international expositions.[5] A high point followed the accommodation between government and church officials that resulted in the announcement of the crowning of Our Lady of Guadalupe, scheduled for October 12,

NON FECIT TALITER OMNI
NATIONI.

Nuestra Señora Santísima: Santa María de
GUADALUPE
Madre y Reina de los Mexicanos.

Tip. Arsacio Vanegas Arroyo, Guatemala 47 México, D. F.

Catholic leaders and Mexico's social elite arranged the crowning of the Virgin of Guadalupe, the patron saint of Mexico, on October 12, 1895. The ceremony used a crown of precious jewels and required papal approval. Officially the government of President Porfirio Díaz ignored the event, but the fact that it occurred indicated the "live-and-let-live" relationship between the church and state. The Virgin, according to church accounts and popular legend, first appeared in December 12, 1531. She became and remains the most powerful religious symbol in the nation. Jean Charlot Collection, University of Hawaii at Manoa Library

1895. This event required the approval of both the pope and the president because public religious celebrations required governmental authorization. Díaz's silence provided tacit approval; behind the scenes, he welcomed the international attention.

The Vatican judged the crowning an indication of the president's goodwill, in part, because the First Lady, Carmen, headed the committee to raise the funds for the holy tiara, fabricated in Paris of gold, silver, rubies, and other precious gems. The coronation attracted bishops from throughout North America, international delegations, and the first families from across Mexico. Thousands attended the parades and ceremonies during the week that concluded with the crowning before the audience of a few hundred that packed the shrine in Tepeyec. Others were allowed to enter after the ceremony to see the crown and banner. Indians and others not attired in modern clothing were not permitted on the basilica grounds on the day of the coronation but had to wait until the following day to offer their devotions to the Virgin.

Sixteen years of political and economic changes began affecting society. The oligarchy of about 3 percent of the population rested on a growing but still minuscule professional class of another 7 percent of the people. The remaining 90 percent of the population made up the lower classes, mostly rural peasantry. This segment included an expanding number of wage earners in textiles, mining, and commercial agriculture. Occupational differentiation existed within the lower class, with market and railroad station vendors, artisans, muleteers, and ox cart drivers that made up the common transportation system in much of the country, water carriers, village money lenders, and many others. The great bulk of the rural lower class engaged in subsistence agriculture, occasionally mixed with seasonal work in mining, commercial agriculture, or railway construction. Newly created service positions such as conductors and ticket collectors on trolleys and railroads, and a few sales clerks in the new department stores, joined the traditional small shop owners and government bureaucrats as the middle sector.

Municipal leaders in Mexico City, San Luis Potosí, Mérida, Puebla, Guadalajara, Querétaro, and other towns adopted new urban practices, modern buildings, and lifestyles. The town clock, usually placed in the central plaza, created a new rhythm of life and work. Porfirian administrators developed paternalistic reforms that intruded into everyday activities. They targeted public health issues (associated primarily with prostitution) and control of vice, vagrancy, and, above all, drunkenness.

They linked the latter with crime, family breakups, low productivity, and poor work discipline. San Lunes (Saint Monday), the holiday for hungover workers, symbolized the problem to elites, who viewed the lower classes as uniquely susceptible to alcohol, thus in need of imposed discipline. Use of traditional pulque came under attack as a distasteful throwback to ancient times. Fresh pulque (which was nonalcoholic) had nutritional value and served as a tonic for the old and infirm. Fermented pulque provided an inexpensive alcoholic beverage, readily available. Mexico City had some 1,600 *pulquerías* in the 1890s, whose fanciful names expressed popular attitudes, including "The Retreat of the Holy Virgin," "The Hang Out of John the Baptist," and, promisingly, "A Night of Delight." By law, the pulquerías closed at 6:00 P.M., but unlicensed vendors supplied pulque at any hour. Employers justified paying workers with script, paper money that could be used only at the company store, on the grounds that such wages could not be spent on pulque or other alcoholic drinks.

Porifiran reformers challenged other activities they considered vices associated with alcohol, such as gambling, prostitution, and loitering in plazas and on street corners. They promoted European and American sports like soccer, baseball, bicycling, and roller skating with the assumption they would mold a lower class dedicated to thrift, sobriety, hard work, and modern hygiene.[6] Public welfare became a federal responsibility as Diaz placed it under the ministry of the interior. Administration reformers, employing the latest management techniques, reconstituted prisons, workshops, hospitals, orphanages, night schools for workers, and other institutions to reproduce supposedly scientific results claimed in Europe. The middle and upper classes enthusiastically adopted social engineering that implied their right to modify lower-class behavior based on their presumed superior understanding of virtue and its results.

The Porfirian era resulted in a good deal of upward and some downward social mobility. Loyal supporters received opportunities to achieve great profits, but many old hacienda families lost out to liberal politics, commercial agriculture, and nascent industry. The Sánchez Navarro fortune, in an extreme example, founded by an energetic priest in Monclova, Coahuila, in the 1760s, eventually encompassed landholdings the size of Portugal. The family's wealth began to decline with the Revolution of Ayutla in 1855 as they resolutely backed the losing Conservatives during the restored republic, when they lost nearly all their properties as the Liberals, led by President Juárez, seized land.

Typical examples of Porfirian success stories included Leopoldo Gómez, a textile merchant, who moved from Puebla to Mexico City to have access to the rail line to Veracruz. As his Mexico City store flourished, he soon developed the family's holdings to include textile mills, tobacco factories, insurance companies, banks, and land.[7] In Monterrey, the Garza-Sada family began the industrialization of the city with the brewing industry. German investors encouraged the new industry, and the family advertised the idea that beer was healthier than the traditional pulque. In Chihuahua, the Terrazas family owed its success to the initial efforts of Luis, a butcher in the 1850s, who bought some land. As a result of the cattle boom of the 1880s, the family properties underwent enormous expansion and became legendary, with approximately 15 million acres with some 400,000 cattle, 100,000 sheep, and 24,000 horses. Profits estimated at half a million dollars from cattle exports led to diversification into banks (including the Guaranty Trust and Banking Company in El Paso, Texas), insurance companies, textile factories, a flour mill, a brewery, and copper mines. The Terrazas bank provided easy credit for family enterprises and on occasion lent money to foreigners, including Alexander Shephard's Batopilas Mining Company and Colonel William Greene's Sierra Madre Land and Lumber Company.

In Coahuila, Evaristo Madero laid the foundation of his family's fortune with cargo wagons that linked San Antonio, Texas with the Mexican towns of Parras, Saltillo, Monterrey, and San Luis Potosí. During the U.S. Civil War his wagons carried Texan cotton to Mexican mills to circumvent the Union embargo. During the Porfirian years, high demand and prices generated ample profits that allowed Evaristo to found the Bank of Nuevo León in Monterrey and invest in land, textile factories, and mines. The family, which competed in copper mining and refining against the United States firms, including the Guggenheim and Rockefeller interests, became one of the ten wealthiest in the nation.[8]

The essential complement to producers came from consumers, who had amazingly expanded choices. The very rich imported European foods and fine wines, German cutlery, exquisite English dinnerware, French cooks, ornamental plants, and Italian gardeners. Outside of the capital city, the arrival of trunks filled with the latest items from London's army and navy catalog or crates from a French department store instantly brought a family social prestige.[9] Mexican consumers found their cultural models in the Parisian *Revue des Deux Mondes*, a biweekly review of European events and letters, Spanish books and periodicals, and the Mexican literary journal *La Repúblic Literaria*, which published foreign articles and poems in translation. Shoppers in the new Palacio de Hierro and Port of Liverpool department stores, modeled on those in Paris and London, could find advice on appropriate consumer behavior in manuals distributed by the store management. In the capital city, a Continental flair could be found at the gaming tables of the socially prominent Jockey Club, where political and financial elite members exhibited their fashions, wealth, and good taste in the European style.

The Porfirian version of Victorian society had critics of its social, economic, and political mores. Francisco Bulnes, a powerful member of Porfirian intellectual circles who served briefly as secretary of foreign affairs, observed that while Diaz's authoritarian rule might have been necessary at one time, the country in the 1890s could be best served by party politics competing within the constitutional framework. Wistano Luis Orozco, a Liberal lawyer who had helped shaped national legislation to reduce corporate landownership, suggested that the government buy lands and distribute it to the desperate rural inhabitants. Both these men thought of themselves as supporters of the government, and their reasoned views reflected some growing concerns for the preservation of the Porfirian system. Social concern received some support from the church as it shifted away from charity toward active attention to social issues, including the well-being and rights of laborers. The papal encyclical *Rerum Novarum* (1891) introduced the need for social justice, and some younger priests, trained in Colegio Padre Pío in the Vatican, returned to Mexico committed to Catholic unions and social programs.

Beyond the loyal opposition, challenges appeared to the Porfirian regime. The president's harsh handling of resistance to his authority remained consistent. Highwaymen and Indian raiders, individuals in some instances forced out of their traditional communities, relied on brigandage as a way to survive as their lifestyles fell victim to national development programs. The international borderline provided sanctuary at times from army and police units on both sides. Such was the case in Rio Grande City, Texas, where Catarino Garza and Francisco Ruiz Sandoval, regarded by the Porfirian government as brigands and by local communities as leaders of an independence movement, issued a call for revolution on Mexican Independence Day, September 15, 1891. Their effort soon fell to army units.

Another example can be seen with Ricardo Flores Magon and his Mexican Liberal Party (the PLM), which appealed to new wage earners in towns, who still had one foot in the countryside often anchored with parents, family, and memories. Initially the PLM claimed to be the heir of earlier Liberals. Ricardo, with his brothers Enrique and Jesús Flores

Magón, challenged the regime through a critical newspaper, *La Regeneración*. After several stints in jail, and the sacking of the newspaper offices, Jesús chose to turn to more moderate forms of opposition, and Ricardo and Enrique decided to continue their struggle from exile. After Ricardo barely escaped assassination and the newspaper office was again wrecked in San Antonio, the two moved to St. Louis, Missouri. They continued distribution of the newspaper by PLM agents, who also attempted to organize supporting groups in Mexico and in U.S. border towns.

The St. Louis junta explained its goals in the Plan of 1906. This pronouncement, in summary, called for fair wages paid in legal currency, decent working conditions for workers, land for agrarians deprived of their properties, restoration of tribal territory to the Yanqui and Mayo peoples, and revitalization of democratic politics. The Porfirian government hired private detectives to harass Ricardo Flores Magon and members of the junta and provide evidence of neutrality law violations to U.S. authorities. Ricardo's politics became increasingly radical at the same that the U.S. government became more concerned with anarchistic politics among immigrants. Ultimately, Ricardo and the PLM became embroiled in the U.S. judicial system.

Economic crises provided a more immediate threat to the Porfirian regime. The worldwide depression in 1906–7 combined with poor harvests to result in strikes concerned with wages and food prices. The international depression revolved around falling silver prices as several nations moved their economies to the gold standard. The demand for the major exports tumbled, to the detriment of the national economy. Oil had been discovered around the port of Tampico, but it had not yet become a high-demand product. General conditions worsened as droughts affecting an already reduced food supply resulted in severe shortages of corn and beans. Workers in mines, factories, and fields faced lower wages and deteriorating living conditions.

The desperate workers in some instances turned to PLM organizers, who had particular success among miners and factory workers. In 1906, in the Sonora copper mining town of Cananea, the workers initiated a strike, in part under PLM leaders, and in 1907, the workers at the Rio Blanco textile mill walked off the job. The strikers protested low and unequal wages (with foreigners in management earning much more than comparable Mexican employees), unsafe working conditions, and, in the textile factory, child and female labor. Both enterprises had foreign majority ownership, and Díaz, at first, saw the strikes as national issues. His favorable disposition toward the workers changed under the barrage of advice from such cabinet members as Governor Ramón Corral of Sonora, who argued that the workers had fallen under the influence of anarchists. Díaz reversed his position and smashed both strikes with army and volunteer forces.

The president, perhaps because of his advanced age, had become increasingly insulated from the people through his confidence in technology and his technocratic advisers. Shaken by the economic downturn and the major strikes, Díaz began to consider his mortality and to seek ways to make his regime his legacy. As a lifelong Liberal whose every achievement rested on his career in arms to protect and promote Liberalism, he found his solution in the political ideology and practices he had championed as a soldier in deed and as president in law.

His thoughts became public in an interview with the U.S. magazine writer James Creelman in 1908. Creelman described the president as an old but energetic warhorse complete with "dark brown eyes that search your soul," "fine ears close to his head...fighting chin,...wide shoulders, deep chest," and a "personality suggestive of singular power and dignity." Describing his successes in fulfilling the promises of liberalism, Díaz told Creelman that he believed the people had developed sober, self-disciplined habits, learned through Porfirian schools, factories, and farms, and had reached the point that he was no longer indispensable. The President said:

> I have waited patiently for the day when the people of the Mexican Republic would be prepared to choose and change their government at every election without danger of armed revolutions and without injury to the national credit or interference with national progress. I believe that day has come.
> He declared that he would not be a candidate in the presidential elections of 1910.[10]

His announcement opened a political campaign. At least four kinds of candidates began to consider the presidential elections based on both their personal ambitions and their casual convictions of how to preserve the social tranquillity and economic expansion after Díaz stepped down. In the northeastern state of Nuevo León, General Bernardo Reyes believed the Porfirian success rested on having a military officer lead the government. In the Veracruz region, General Félix Díaz, nephew of the president, explained the regime's longevity to having a Díaz family member as president. In Sonora, Governor Ramón Corral found the Porfirian success in tough-minded administration, such as that of a frontier governor. In the capital city, the Científicos believed the social application of technology had maintained the regime, but they remained uncertain of the appropriate candidate.

Two additional opinions on the political actions necessary to preserve Porfirian achievements appeared in book form. In Mexico City, Andrés Molina Enriquez focused on the rural land consolidation of the 1890s as the greatest danger to the nation as it stripped property from smallholders and reduced food production for commercial agricultural expansion. Molina Enriquez did not envision himself a presidential candidate, but his conclusions expressed in *Los Grandes Problemas Nacionales* (1909) became guiding principles for the first half of the twentieth century. In Coahuila, the youngest son of the powerful but out of favor Madero family, Francisco, stated in a widely circulated book on the presidential selection that the preservation of Porfirian successes would be possible with the peaceful transfer of presidential power and that this could only occur through democratic elections. His arguments in *La Successión Presidencial en 1910* laid the basis for his presidential campaign. The book went through several editions, each one a little more daring, until Francisco Madero finally advocated the replacement of Porfirio Diaz.

The proponents of these different political positions, except for Madero, acted with circumspection, waiting to see if President Díaz would indeed not run for reelection. Within months, Díaz allowed himself to be persuaded by various groups to reverse his position and accept the nomination for the presidency in the 1910 election. Hanging back allowed Corral to become the vice presidential nominee (a concession by the eighty-year-old Díaz that he might not survive an entire term) and enabled the Científicos and others to maintain their positions in the Porfirian circle. On the other hand, General Reyes had gone beyond the chain of command. Díaz, in short order, sent Reyes traveling the globe to review military modernization programs. This assignment meant he would lack the year's residence before elections required of all candidates. The president ignored Madero, whose reputation as a dilettante agriculturalist and practicing Spiritualist appeared to rule him out as a serious contender.

Madero understood democracy to mean the creation of political parties with declared principles. He initiated tours of the country to create local clubs of what he called the Anti-Reelectionist Party, with the promise of a national nominating convention in the summer of 1910. For the most part, Porfirian governors and *jefes politicos* followed the example of the president and ignored Madero, but a few of the more autocratic administrators broke up the Anti-Reelectionist organizational meetings, harassed speakers, and, in a few cases, even jailed local party officers. In the latter case, it appears to have resulted because, particularly in the northern states, the Anti-Reelectionists revived PLM groups to create their local committees.

To no one's surprise, at their national nominating convention, the Anti-Reelectionists selected Francisco Madero as their presidential candidate. He spent the summer of 1910 campaigning for the office. The unlikely candidate presented a totally different image than Diaz. Short of stature, with a high-pitched voice, somewhat portly, and clearly a member of the privileged class, he represented those able to take advantage of the new economic opportunities offered by Liberalism after the war with the United States. He advocated structural changes to redress the political system so that elected officials could legislate fundamental social and economic changes. Populist leaders misinterpreted his intentions to work for the lower classes. His campaign created expectations that he had not intended.

President Díaz gave little time to the presidential election campaign. His attention during the summer of 1910 focused on the celebration of the centennial of national independence, which reached a climax on September 16. In the midst of these preparations and precursory events, the presidential elections approached, and Díaz decided to take no chances with Madero. He had the latter placed under house arrest in San Luis Potosí, where he was campaigning. The alleged felony charges made Madero ineligible for election to office. Voting occurred without incident. Officials reported that Madero received some votes that had to be discounted because of his indictment and also announced that Porfirio Díaz had been reelected with an overwhelming number of votes.

Madero acted, but the president again ignored Madero's actions as he focused on the upcoming celebration. Madero in disguise fled to New Orleans, Louisiana, and then San Antonio, Texas. Safely out of the country, he issued a statement purportedly written in San Luis Potosí to avoid violation of U.S. neutrality laws. The Plan of San Luis Potosí called on members of the Anti-Reelectionist Party to reconstitute themselves as revolutionaries and invited other Mexicans to join them in overthrowing the Porfirian government. In secret circulars, Madero announced the revolution would begin at 1:00 P.M. on November 20, 1910.

For Mexicans in general, especially the capital city administration, the fall of 1910 brought a series of major inaugurations of new buildings, monuments, and institutions to commemorate independence.[11]

Celebrating the centennial of independence on September 16, 1910, government organizers staged a parade of national history. The procession began with the Aztec civilization and featured marchers dressed as warriors carrying the emperor Montezuma. Indigenous peoples refused to participate in a display of their conquest. Crowds of spectators flowed into the street, even as the mounted constabulary tried to clear the parade route. L. V. Garcia, *Gran desfile historico, Emperador Moctezuma,* September 15, 1910; The Getty Research Institute, Los Angeles (98.R.104)

The celebration moved toward the September 16 climax with parades and speeches that championed the century of independence, and the nation's survival of civil and foreign wars. It drew official and unofficial visitors from Europe, the United States, Latin America, and Asia, particularly, Japan. Through it all, Díaz, as the elderly general president, remained slightly remote as the national symbol, the patriarchal patriot.

The Díaz regime still basked in the afterglow of the centennial celebrations on November 20, as a few insurrectionary battles took place in distant Chihuahua. Generally, the administration, including the president, gave little attention to Madero and his insurgents, overlooking the widespread popular demands that soon would ignite into a national revolution.

CHAPTER SIX

Revolution, 1910–1946

The call for revolution on November 20, 1910, to overthrow the three-decades-old regime of General Porfirio Díaz came from defeated presidential candidate Francisco Madero, an exile in the United States. His manifesto received little attention from those who opposed the government and even less from its supporters, who still basked in the glow of the extravagant celebration of the centennial of independence. Madero's followers, Pasqual Orozco Jr. and Pancho Villa, won minor victories against federal troops in the remote mountains of distant Chihuahua, and the revolution sputtered to life. Mexico City remained placid and the national administration complacent in response to the faraway uprising.

President Díaz ordered troops north to smash the insurrection, and they nearly did with a victory at Nuevas Casas Grandes, Chihuahua, in December 1910, in which federal troops wounded Madero, who had taken command. Madero quickly relinquished military authority back to Orozco and Villa, who held the rebels together. Despite the loss, the insurrection expanded by fits and starts, as volunteers arrived daily in the north and, in other regions, local rebels took up arms in Madero's name, but with their own goals, such as Emiliano Zapata in Morelos.

In April 1911, the rebels in Chihuahua managed to isolate the federal army in Ciudad Juárez. For three days, rebels carried out fierce house-to-house fighting, watched by a holiday crowd of spectators across the Rio Grande in El Paso, to capture the city. The victory gave them a border port for the shipment of guns and ammunition and an even greater public relations victory. New rebel groups began to appear almost daily. Shaken by the defeat of his troops, Díaz ordered negotiations with Madero that concluded in May 1911 with the Treaties of Ciudad Juárez. In the accords, the president agreed to resign and go into exile. Díaz, his family, and many of his closest advisers sailed for Paris in May 1911, bringing an end to the thirty-five years of Porfirian rule and nineteenth-century politics.[1]

The rebels who seized power in 1911 represented a young generation that would dominate the country until 1946. As individuals, they came from different class and ethnic backgrounds; many became rebels because they had recently lost their political independence and liveli-hood or feared they would. They included subsistence farmers (*campe-sinos*) who had lost their communal properties, independent highlanders (*rancheros*) who had lost their lands, craftsmen who had lost their trades, commercial agriculturists who had lost markets, and small miners who had lost their enterprise to corporations. Others included provincial elites who had lost their political influence and indigenous peoples denied social and economic access to modernizing programs.

They shared a commitment to create a nation that offered social mobility to all its citizens, the opportunity to participate in their government, the prospect of economic justice, and the promise of legal equality. They all intended to achieve these goals by limiting the economic activities, political influence, and ethnic prejudices of for-eigners (especially mining, railroad, and commercial entrepreneurs) and by reducing the role of three domestic groups—the capital city bourgeoisie, the Catholic Church hierarchy, and the commercial agri-culturalists (the owners of large estates that produced export crops such as coffee and sugarcane).

In the revolutionary struggle, the rebel resort to violence established a pattern that continued for at least three decades. Several leaders, notably Pancho Villa, Emiliano Zapata, and above all Lázaro Cárdenas, became national heroes, and in some cases international celebrities. They shared a brash nonchalance about death that came from an under-standing that beyond their lives, they had little to lose. Their achieve-ment came as these populist rebels initiated and administered the world's first social revolution.

Rebels, both men and women, risked their lives for a better life, and for an exciting adventure. While fighting for their demands for farm land, workers' rights, political participation, and basic needs for health, education, and housing, the rebels experienced a wider world. For the first time, many rode trains, mounted horses, even drove cars, and saw new places, especially the national capital with the president's office, tall buildings, departmental stores, and posh restaurants; as long as they survived, they grabbed shirts, boots, spoons, saddles, or whatever they wanted as loot. From the beginning, they also met other Mexicans from across the republic.

Violence had a scattered, local character that swept back and forth across the country. The battles and regimes moved in kaleidoscopic fashion, as the first phase of the revolution under Francisco Madero (1910–13) fell to the counterrevolution of military dictator Victoriano Huerta that ignited the Constitutionalist revolution (1913–14) of

In 1913, Pancho Villa directed his revolutionary army southward toward the capital city, using the railroads. Men and women rebels made boxcars their homes, cooking and sleeping atop and inside the train cars. Women, called soldaderas, fought alongside the men or worked in the commissaries and medical service and as morale boosters. Hugo Brehme, *Zeltlager der revolutionären Truppen auf den Dächern von Eisenbahn Wagon in México,* ca. 1914; The Getty Research Institute, Los Angeles (98.R.5)

Venustiano Carranza, Pancho Villa, Alvaro Obregón, and Emiliano Zapata, followed by civil war once Huerta fled as the Constitutionalist leaders divided against each other (1914–16) and invasion by U.S. Marines (at Veracruz and Tampico) and soldiers (the Pershing Punitive Expedition, named for General John J. Pershing, in Chihuahua).

The revolutionaries fought some large-scale battles that featured the deep trenches, barbed wire, and machine guns modeled on the contemporary European warfare, but more frequently small armies appeared suddenly on horseback or on freight trains and fought skirmishes that ended with the victors executing the losing officers and often allowing the enlisted men to change sides. Nomadic bands roamed the countryside, pillaging the great estates and small settlements and looting homes, towns, and mines. Women formed part of these armies as combatants, sometimes as officers, and as camp followers who provided the commissary and medical treatment for the troops.[2] The dangers of remaining in the countryside quickly drove families—often just women and children because the men had joined the upheaval—to flee to the greater security of towns and cities.

The victors established presidential regimes beginning in 1916 that survived their terms, only to fall to assassination and rebellion as a means of succession in 1920, 1923, and 1928. Antirevolutionary Catholics took the field from 1926 to 1929, and again briefly in 1933. As a result, all of the revolution's early leaders—Francisco Madero (1913), Emiliano Zapata (1919), Venuestiano Carranza (1920), Pancho Villa (1923), Alvaro Obregón (1928), and a dozen more—were murdered. They joined one in seven of the nation's population who died in the fighting, from wounds, or from disease or deprivation or who fled into exile as result of the revolution in just the decade after 1910 (nearly 2 million people in all).[3] More died in the decades leading to 1940.

The revolution's achievements seemed minimal in the first decade, with the outstanding exception of the writing of the constitution of 1917, which offered four major provisions. These articles initiated land reform to restore village lands and provide lands to those who worked them, while claiming national ownership of subsoil and water rights; announced the most advanced labor code in the world for workers, with an emphasis on wages, safety, and unionization; prohibited monopolies, in an effort to make food, housing, education, and health care available to everyone; and attempted to restrict the Catholic Church to religious issues, nationalizing all church properties including temples, eliminating all political rights of priests, and expelling foreign prelates. (This last episode received novelistic treatment in Graham Greene's *Power and the Glory*.)

Implementing these constitutional provisions required enabling legislation and presidential backing, so that Alvaro Obregón (president, 1920–24) focused on land reform and labor organization, Plutarco Calles (president, 1924–28) initiated strict anticlerical enabling legislation, and Lázaro Cárdenas (president, 1934–40) administered a comprehensive campaign for all of the constitutional provisions. Tying together the constitutional social initiatives was a commitment to the ideal of the mestizo, the mixture of ethnicities into one nationality, race, and culture that Secretary of Education José Vasconcelos termed the Cosmic Race. Internationally famous muralists, particularly Diego Rivera, hired by Vasconcelos, gave artistic expression to these revolutionary campaigns.

Obregón occupied the presidency from 1920 to 1924, joined by his close advisers from Sonora, Adolfo de la Huerta (interim president, 1920) and Plutarco Calles (president, 1924–28; *jefe maximo* [maximum leader], 1928–36). The three brought a commitment to social programs that would rebuild the national government and revolutionize the society and the economy. Obregón attempted to reduce national violence, redistribute agricultural lands to the nation's peasants, and revitalize government finances by using oil production for social programs, especially education.

Obregon's agrarian program focused on restoring land to villages (often properties that Porfirian commercial agricultural entrepreneurs had seized), most often as community holdings, but worked by individual families. In a program delayed by bureaucracy, counterclaims to titles from various villages, and large estate owners, the Obregón regime nevertheless successfully distributed properties to 128,907 actual recipients (in the system, many communities received tentative grants of land, but the actual titles took years to obtain).[4] The land reform often contributed to the rural violence, as villagers invaded properties in efforts to reclaim them, and estate owners hired gunmen, called white guards, to preempt any land invaders.

The revolution's most successful general, President Obregón, also faced difficulties with the revolutionary army. He intended to reduce violence and return to more tranquil times by reducing the size of the army, especially the number of generals (there were 116 generals of division), by retiring officers, placing others on the inactive list, and discharging troops. As a first step, he ordered the registration of all revolutionary soldiers with their ranks. Rather than spending time sorting out things, he declared that if "someone said he is a general, he is a general." Once he had the officers identified, he began placing them on the retirement list, using what he referred to as a "cannon blast of pesos," that is, bonuses to encourage retirement. Consequently, Obregón spent close to half of the national budget on the revolution's soldiers during his presidency, with the lowest expenditure 33.6 percent of the 1923 budget. The annual expenditure in millions of pesos was as follows: 1920: 63.8; 1921: 120.0; 1923: 79.2; and 1924: 117.8. Remarkably, these payments to the military were reductions in national spending from previous administrations.[5]

Foreign nations, particularly the United States and Great Britain, expressed grave concerns about the 1917 constitutional provisions that made landowning a social responsibility rather than an inherent right and that returned ownership of all subsurface rights to the national government. Representatives of these foreign governments wanted protection of the properties in Mexico owned by their citizens. These foreigners held titles to commercial agricultural lands, mines, and oil fields.

Another group of foreign bankers clamored for resolution of the Mexican debt they held in bonds. Obregón's foreign minister, Alberto Pani, carried out masterful negotiations that resulted in agreement that the government would not attempt to enforce the constitution's provision retroactively on properties on which efforts to develop the economic potential of the lands had occurred (called "positive acts"), but land left fallow faced expropriation. Pani and his colleagues brilliantly divided the foreigners by proposing a tax on foreign oil producers that would be used to pay debts to the foreign bankers and bondholders. This agreement, with some discrepancies on each side, resulted in the Bucareli Agreements of 1923, followed by U.S. recognition of the revolutionary government.

Obregón named José Vasconcelos secretary of the newly created Ministry of Public Education. Vasconcelos brought frenetic energy to his office, with nonstop programs to teach the nation's peoples about their history, culture, and heritage. He inspired public murals (thirty-six in the Obregón years), civic sculptures, rural schools, capital city open-air painting classes, and national collections of indigenous clothing and musical traditions. The president invested what he could in the educational programs, and his 1922 and 1923 expenditures of 13 and 15 percent, respectively, of the national budget were the first ever commitment of funds in double digits for national education.[6]

Obregón's regime and the Sonoran administrations that followed promoted cultural programs to give visual displays of the new society, provide dramatic statements of government programs, and offer memorable expressions of revolutionary nationality. Taken together these efforts aimed at establishing the legitimacy of the new order, identifying the appropriate historical legacies, and celebrating the revolutionary society. Officially sponsored activities included new monuments to revolutionary heroes, parades for new revolutionary holidays, and the celebration of the centennial of the achievement of independence (1921) that featured the crowning of María Bibiana Uribe from Necaxa, Puebla, as the India Bonita (in a beauty contest theoretically restricted to indigenous women). The celebration of independence resulted in a variety of classic and revue theater performances, opera, ballet, *orquestas típicas*, folk dances, and the Exhibition of Popular Arts, which later toured the United States.[7] The celebration of popular culture and history opened the revolutionary society to the outside world.

This openness to social programs developed elsewhere gave the Mexican Revolution its unique character. During the Obregon years, the influence of American John Dewey, Chilean Ménez Bravo, and

Hired by the Ministry of Public Education, Luis Márquez went into rural Mexico in the 1920s to photograph the indigenous peoples whom the revolutionary leaders expected to be assimilated into the new society. He concentrated on Indian women, such as this Otomí woman from rural Hidalgo, and also collected their traditional dress. Both his photographs and the costumes were quickly used by painters hired to illustrate popular calendars given away as advertising by tequila producers, bars, and restaurants. Otomi Maiden, Mexico by Luis Márquez from the Luis Márquez Collection, The Wittliff Collections, Texas State University-San Marcos

Peruvian Vivar V. Patrón appeared in the new educational programs. Women in the Yucatán, who pushed for female political rights and social programs, drew inspiration from Jane Addams, and Governor Pedro Alvarado eventually invited her to come from Chicago to the Maya peninsula and consult on social programs there. The energetic and imaginative programs drew foreign artists, writers, journalists, photographers, folklorists, and the curious to the capital, where many joined in what historian Mauricio Tonorio-Trillo has labeled the nation's "Cosmopolitan Summer" of revolution.[8] Anita Brenner, Carleton Beals, Katherine Anne Porter, and Francis Toor joined the Mexican artistic circle that included Diego Rivera, Miguel Covarrubías, Moisés Sáenz, and Dr. Atl, who promoted both Mexico and its revolution.

The young revolutionaries who came to the capital and carried out these reforms took time to enjoy life as well. The northerners wanted familiar music, sought out romance (sometimes with the children of old Porfirians), attended theaters to see both Mexican and Hollywood movies, and raced around town in imported Hudson and Ford motor cars. At home they listened to recordings of music from the north and across the nation. Successful because of their military experience, they brought the same improvisational pragmatism to the capital. From Obregon down through the ranks and across the bureaucracy, the revolutionaries sought ways to accomplish their goals and to enjoy the good life as they understood it. To some extent the new urban culture reflected the cosmopolitan fashions such as those of the flapper, known in Mexico as the *pelona* (the baldy, for her short hair), but more than anything it resulted from flouting old social roles.

The years of revolutionary reconstruction saw increased urbanization combined with developing media of radio, recordings, films, and comic books that reflected and shaped the new, more open city life that was less caste-bound than the previous society. No more obvious expression of changing social propriety existed than displays of public affection. The intimate lovers' kiss without regard for the audience could be found everywhere, in the park, on the street corner, in restaurants, and on public transportation. During the Porfirian years commonly the peasant workers were expected to kiss the hand of the hacendado overlords who had seized the land. In the new revolutionary era, urban and liberated society found its most personal expression in the public kiss.

The presidency of Plutarco E. Calles (1924–28) continued Obregón's radical remaking of the society. The president added to programs of land reform and public education his personal emphasis on anticlericalism and unionization. His expansion of social programs benefited from Obregón's reduction of army budgets and the unsuccessful 1923 military rebellion in support of the presidency of Adolfo de la Huerta. The latter resulted in numerous deaths, executions, and retirements of senior officers. Calles spent the increased federal monies on programs for land distribution, anticlerical campaigns through the schools, and assistance to working groups. He succeeded in more than doubling the number of acres (8 million) that Obregón had redistributed (3 million acres) and continued the emphasis on land grants to small families.

Emulating the Obregón programs aimed at solving social problems, Calles expanded the rural education missions and established the Department of Public Health. The health campaign not only featured the major smallpox vaccination campaign in 1926 but also initiated health inspections of food and beverage production. The agency determined to teach children proper hygiene practices and worked with several antialcohol campaigns. Embedded in both education and hygienic programs under Calles was a virulent anticlericalism. Calles intended to create a secular society, free from both what he regarded as Catholic mumbo jumbo and superstition, and the economic and political influence exercised by priests. His campaign encouraged state governors to make civic use of church buildings, restrict the public presence of priests, and instigate campaigns to destroy religious icons. Particularly in the states of Tabasco under Tomás Garrido Canabal (1920–35) and Sonora under the president's son, Rodolfo Elías Calles (1931–35), the anticlerical campaign took on a feverish character, with youngsters organized to burn holy images, destroy church windows, and harry the religious in every way imaginable.

The Calles anticlerical campaign threatened Catholics, both priests and believers, and for many it proved to be the last straw. Substantial numbers of both priests and laity supported social revolutionary programs with a role for the church (these individuals organized Catholic Social Action), while others remained quite conservative or reactionary in their beliefs. Once Calles initiated his policies, the more activist priests and parishioners organized Catholic Defense groups to protect their religious communities. These groups, ignoring dictates from the bishops and archbishops, soon began to stockpile arms and ammunition. Calles's hostility to the church met an equally hostile reaction from Archbishop José Mora y del Río of Mexico City, who declared that Catholics could not accept the constitution. His jeremiad provoked Calles to action, ordering the registration of all priests, among other restrictions. In response, bishops declared a church strike, beginning in 1926, which closed temples, suspended masses, and ended sacraments.

The strike ignited a civil war called the Cristero Rebellion. More military Catholics through their defense leagues began a series of attacks against the agents of the government, especially rural schoolteachers and soldiers. They murdered and wounded teachers and dynamited a troop train. Particularly in the western states, but elsewhere as well, the Cristeros provoked brutal attacks and retaliation on both sides. The bishops soon fled to safety in exile as lay Catholics battled federal troops and state militias.

In the midst of the Cristero fighting, revolutionary leaders became divided over the question of presidential succession. Former president Obregón had decided that the nation needed strong leadership and that only he could defeat the Cristeros. Consequently, he and his supporters pressed congress to amend the constitutional—and hallowed—revolutionary principle of "no reelection" to "no immediate reelection." Obregón then won election to a second term, with an inauguration set for December 1928. While some revolutionaries, including Calles, had misgivings about this succession, the Cristeros were appalled at the prospect of an alternation in office between Obregón and Calles. Attempts on Obregón's life followed. As the president-elect motored to the bullring with three friends, a car pulled alongside, and a passenger unsuccessfully hurled a bomb at them. Shortly afterward at an afternoon dinner in a swanky San Angel restaurant celebrating Obregón's successful election, a sketch artist hired to draw caricatures of the guests approached the president-elect, drew a pistol, and shot him to death.

The assassination and earlier attempts gave the Cristeros martyrs. The Jesuit priest Padre Miguel Pro, who conspired to murder Obregón, and José de León Toral, who assassinated him, were both convicted and died before military firing squads. Padre Pro recently was made one of the saints of the church, along with other Cristero priests killed during the rebellion. The fighting continued for three years until, finally, the struggle sputtered out, as civil and church negotiators agreed to recognize the integrity of the other's position. The revolutionaries continued their social programs, and the church resumed its religious activities. Certainly, fanatics remained on both sides, and the few ferocious outbreaks of accusations and violence in the future notwithstanding, government leaders recognized the national culture was encrusted in Catholicism, and church leaders understood that the revolutionary leaders and their programs dominated politics. Both now understood that neither the revolutionary regime nor the Roman Catholic Church was going away.

Running parallel to the Cristero struggle, revolutionary efforts to legitimate the national regime continued. The murder of Obregón ended talk of presidential reelection. In 1929, Calles moved to solve the succession difficulty with two major steps: the creation of an official party that would contain struggles over candidates and a revision of the single presidential term to six years. The Partido Nacional Revolucionario (PNR; National Revolutionary Party) brought together revolutionaries, including military officers, agrarian leaders, labor organizers, and government agents from public health, education, and finance. The party, in theory and most of the time in practice, contained conflicts among the revolutionaries, selected candidates for offices, disciplined voters, and manipulated ballots cast to ensure victories. This organization became the official party that (with two later name changes) dominated the national government until the presidential election of 2000. The creation of a six-year term reduced the number of presidential campaigns and gave individuals more time to develop programs.

The immediate political demand was for a president to replace Obregón. The first six-year term reflected the intense political rivalries confronting the party leaders. Calles remained a formidable presence, and despite illness and foreign travel, he exercised considerable influence on the government using the unofficial title *jefe maximo*. Emilio Portes Gil (1928–30) replaced Obregón and carried out social programs as he arranged for new presidential elections. Although often viewed as the cat's-paw of Calles, in fact, he initiated major land reforms, defused college student strikes by arranging for university autonomy, and, failing to arrange the withdrawal of U.S. troops from Nicaragua, gave asylum and an agricultural property to rebel leader Augusto Sandino. His interest in the entertainment industry led to his promotion of the mariachi band from his home state of Tamaulipas in national films, including the classic *Alla en el Rancho Grande*.

Elections placed General Pascual Ortiz Rubio in office, but an assassination attempt by Daniel Flores on the afternoon of his inauguration, in which both Rubio and his wife received gunshot wounds, disrupted his administration from its beginning. Despite intense interrogation, Flores refused to identify any coconspirators (he later died without explanation in his cell). General Eulogio Ortiz nevertheless ordered the arrest, torture, and then secret execution of sixty supporters of José Vasconcelos, who had stood as the opposition presidential candidate. The murder victims were discovered about a month later, and the event became widely known as the Massacre of Topilejo. The president also ordered an armored car for his personal use. The car, complete with inch-thick reinforced windows, protected the president against would-be assassins but could not shield him from associates

Communist Party members, opposed to President Alvaro Obregón's support for other unions, demanded greater government attention to the working classes rather than agrarian issues. The photographer Tina Modotti, an Italian member of the intellectual community of foreigners such as Edwin Weston and Mexicans such as Diego Rivera, made photography a political medium. Tina Modotti, *Untitled*, 1923; gelatin silver print; 2 15/16 in. x 3 7/8 in. (7.46 cm x 9.84 cm); San Francisco Museum of Modern Art, Purchase through a gift of the Art Supporting Foundation, John "Launny" Steffens, Sandra Lloyd, Shawn and Brook Byers, Mr. and Mrs. George F. Jewett, Jr., and anonymous donors

who looked past him to former president Calles for leadership. As a result, the president felt Calles exercised undue interference in his government. Constant political disruption was underscored by the economic difficulties that resulted from the world depression. As a result, barely two years after his inauguration, Ortiz Rubio resigned and went into exile in the United States.

General Abelardo Rodríguez finished the term (1932–34), and despite the economic challenges caused by the world depression, such as the repatriation of an estimated 500,000 Mexicans and Mexican Americans by the United States, the president carried out successful programs. Determined to eliminate internal conflicts, he notified all cabinet members that they had to have his approval for all decisions. He supported the building improvement programs of financial minister

Alberto Pani, especially the completion of the Bellas Artes Building and, in an effort to save the iron cupola from being sold as scrap, the conversion of the half-finished Porfirian congress building into the Monument to the Revolution. Rodríguez also initiated an effort to establish minimum wages for all workers across the nation in the face of the world depression. He did not reach his goal of four pesos a day but made progress and reached nearly half that in the capital. He also continued the land reform efforts, despite the economic contraction caused by the depression.

All three of these two-year presidents—Portes Gil, Ortíz, and Rodríguez—came to office with experience as military commanders and successful state governors of Tamaulipas, Michoacan, and Baja California del Norte, respectively. Despite the long shadow of Calles, they proved capable of running their own administrations.

As the nation approached the 1934 presidential election, the PNR called for a convention to establish a six-year plan to guide the next chief executive. Interim president Rodríguez had a major role in shaping the document by the appointment of the committee that wrote the first draft. Delegates at the PNR convention in Querétaro revised the document, without completely redoing it. The party then backed the official candidate, Lázaro Cárdenas, another revolutionary general and state governor. Cárdenas had a populist sensibility that resulted in a peripatetic campaign, visiting major cities and remote villages across the nation. He traveled with mariachis, and in addition to music, he listened to local needs rather than lectured voters on their duties.

The Cárdenas presidency (1934–1940) became the apogee of social revolution as he insisted on the implementation of constitutional provisions, especially land reform (he redistributed 4,958, 203 hectares during his term) and labor organization.[9] He continued to travel widely and became the first president to make use of the radio as a political tool, giving regular talks to his fellow citizens. During his campaign and after, he actively promoted the rights of all citizens and had committed himself to extending voting rights to women. The suffrage campaign was put off due to an economic crisis. Foreign oil company officials challenged the Cárdenas governmental programs, and when they refused to abide by judicial decisions against them, Cárdenas nationalized the oil industry on March 17, 1938—an event widely proclaimed as the nation's declaration of economic independence. Despite boycotts by U.S., British, and Dutch refineries and shippers, the Mexicans organized a national corporation (PEMEX) that remains a powerful oil producer today.

As European events cast a shadow across Mexico, Cárdenas became a leading spokesman in favor of the Spanish Republicans, who fought the army and Conservatives (along with their Nazi German and Italian Fascist assistance) in the Spanish Civil War (1936–39). After their defeat, he welcomed exiles and orphans from Spain. Moreover, the Spanish Civil War deeply influenced Cárdenas as he considered his successor. The left-wing members of the official party, now renamed the Partido Revolucionario Mexicano (PRM; Mexican Revolutionary Party), favored the president's mentor, Francisco J. Mújica, the general who had preceded him as governor of Michoacán, chaired the 1917 Constitutional Convention, served as a member of his cabinet, and helped promote revolutionary efforts in Venezuela and several Central American countries. The president worried that a militant leftist candidate would provoke the militant right to action and result in civil war, as it had in Spain. He decided to choose a more moderate candidate and turned to his longtime subordinate General Manuel Avila Camacho from Puebla. The latter faced a major campaign challenge from General Juan A. Almazán, backed by business and church leaders on the right, but the PRM carried the election. Cárdenas left office as the epitome of the revolution; in part this reflected the fact that the largest number of like-minded revolutionary veterans from the countryside (80 percent) made up his government.[10]

As a former president, Cárdenas adopted a senior statesman's demeanor, but members of his administration continued to press for his policies. Out of the public view, the onetime First Lady, Amalia Solórzano de Cárdenas, became increasingly active in politics. The public first saw her in public affairs as a prominent member of the Aid Committee for Children of the Spanish People. She remained active in official party politics until 1952, when many of Cárdenas's colleagues organized the Party of the Revolution and backed Miguel Henríquez Guzmán in an unsuccessful bid for president. Because Solórzano de Cárdenas took an active role in the campaign for Henríquez Guzmán, it was widely believed that the former president backed him as well.

Avila Camacho succeeded Cárdenas from 1940 to 1946. Although often portrayed as a more conservative president by choice, in fact his ability to carry out social programs was severely restricted by World War II. His regime worked in concert with the United States in support of the Allies, and Mexico declared war against Germany, Italy and Japan in the spring of 1942. Mexicans provided vast amounts of needed raw materials for the war effort, especially oil, lead, zinc, cottonseed oil, and mahogany. Air Force Squadron 201, based in the Philippines in

1944, flew support for the Allied invasions of islands moving toward Japan. Many additional Mexicans joined the U.S. armed forces and fought in both Europe and Asia. No separate statistics were kept of Mexican, Mexican American, or Latino members of the U.S. armed forces, but the total is estimated at 250,000 to 500,000, or 2.3 to 4.7 percent of the total.[11] When the war ended, Mexicans played a leading role in the creation of the United Nations, especially of the children's organization, UNICEF.

Avila Camacho, despite the demands of the war, pushed forward programs to provide social security for workers. At first limited in scope to the capital, then reaching other cities, nevertheless the Social Security Institute began to provide an essential health care safety net to the public. The government continued the effort to grapple with issues of potable water, sewage disposal, accessible transport, and basic literacy. The latter problem resulted in a campaign under the motto "Each one teach one." Those individuals who taught several others to read received certificates and other awards. In some cases, social centers such as the one in Oaxaca City offered women the opportunity to use sewing machines in exchange for attending literacy classes.

Revolutionary programs with their social and economic goals shaped this period, but other major developments had an impact on the society. These were the increasing pattern of urbanization, especially to the capital city; the successful public health campaigns that resulted in rapid population growth; and the adoption of technology that provided the development of mass media. The era from 1920 through 1946 became the golden age of radio, records, and movies, centered in the rapidly growing Mexico City.

Mexico City and other cities, during the war years, found themselves overwhelmed by housing, water, and transportation needs. The demands of the war limited spending on these needs, which came to constitute the immediate problems of the postwar years. The success of public health programs meant that many more Mexicans survived their first year of life, reached adulthood, and lived longer. This happy development increased the burden on schools, public services, and employment. The number of literate individuals vastly increased, but the percentage of illiterate people remained high because of the population increase.

Shortly after the end of the war, Mexico had become an urban nation—population statistics show slightly more than half of the people lived in urban areas by 1960.[12] This change required new approaches by future governmental administrations and shifts in the revolutionary

The Zócalo (central plaza), the preeminent public space in the national capital, brought together members of revolutionary society, who expressed modern, working-class identity in overalls, although some of the rural migrants continued to wear sombreros, and women adopted modern clothing. The motorcycle offers a preview of coming traffic jams and air pollution that soon came to plague the city. Tina Modotti, *Zócalo* (Mexico City Square), ca. 1926–1929. Gelatin silver print; 2 5/8 in. x 3 3/4 in.; San Francisco Museum of Modern Art, Purchase through a gift of the Art Supporting Foundation, John "Launny" Steffens, Sandra Lloyd, Shawn and Brook Byers, Mr. and Mrs. George F. Jewett, Jr., and anonymous donors

programs. The urban nation shaped the national culture, with the advent of radio, recordings, movies, and comic books. The focus of this new mass media was urban life and its problems, and a romantic nostalgia for a rural past that never existed. Cosmopolitan nightlife with its mambo rhythms and bolero ballads had a major audience of those who lived in cities and those who dreamed of doing so. For those who missed the country, ranchero music and mariachi bands created a wistful rural refuge. Music blared everywhere, and as the nation prepared for a new president in 1946, it heard the popular Veracuz song "La Bamba," rewritten to promote the presidential campaign of the official candidate, Miguel Alemán. Of course, he won.

CHAPTER SEVEN

Revolution for Middling Mexicans and Its End, 1938–1982

T hree major transitions from 1938 to 1982 reshaped national life in revolutionary society. The first saw the switch of official government programs from a rural to an urban focus, with the promotion of industry and services in place of the agrarian redistribution of land and water rights. The second came with the emergence of a new generation of city-reared, civilian, college-educated leaders who, beginning in 1946, replaced the rural-born revolutionary veterans who preceded them. The third resulted from the accelerated migration from the countryside to the city, not just to the capital city but to Guadalajara, Monterrey, and Puebla, and to resort towns, especially Acapulco.

The change in generations affected politics but was not accompanied, as many have argued, by a return of conservative politicians who reclaimed the government. Rather, it resulted at first from the pragmatism of President Lázaro Cárdenas, with his determination to do the best possible for his people, and then with the emergence of new leaders who benefited from the revolution, especially from improved working conditions and opportunities for education. The middle sectors—not really a class and certainly not all identified with bourgeois behavior—followed these programs, which they viewed as theirs. The position of many of these middling groups was summed up as "It's Our Turn Now." This motto reflected the view that government reform programs had already provided for the agrarians and for the workers, and it was now time to do something for middling Mexicans.[1] This program that aimed at the city and increasingly the middle sectors rested in the hands of the revolutionary generation from 1938 to 1946. It later became the primary focus of the new generation that came to power in 1952.

Before the shift to urban programs could make much headway, Mexico became embroiled in the global conflict. On May 22, 1942, Mexican entered World War II with a commitment to a world free of the aggression and imperialism of Nazi Germany, Fascist Italy, and militarist Japan. These three Axis nations threatened the revolutionary programs in Mexico and other nations, especially the Soviet Union. Mexicans participated as a nation in the Pacific battles with an air force squadron, and individually with many Mexicans enlisted in the U.S. military. Mexicans served with valor and won many citations, including the Medal of Honor.

On the home front, Mexicans experienced changes through the participation of women in many occupations, including a woman's parachute nurses unit, expanded roles in management at the telephone company where they traditionally worked only as operators, and in much larger numbers in teaching and journalism. They also worked beside men with the shifting of the economy to produce essential products for the war effort. Farmers enthusiastically changed their crops from corn to cottonseed to produce oil for use as a lubricant and other products. The agriculture industry's efforts in that direction even resulted in the prospect of famine, only averted with the shipment of corn from the United States and Canada. Mexico also provided silver, lead, and other minerals to the Allies, along with mahogany used in the construction of patrol boats and airplanes. Mexicans went to the United States to work in agriculture, war industries, and railroads under a guest system. These individuals, called braceros, made a fundamental contribution to the war effort, as they and U.S. women became the primary workforce because U.S. men had been mobilized into the military.

Once the Allies, including Mexico, secured victory, Mexicans found that they both benefited and suffered in the international situation of the postwar years. The nation and its people initially benefited as the savings forced on both the government and individuals provided a great deal of capital for major national construction programs and individual consumer purchases. Mexico emerged as a leader in the tier of nations just behind the allied powers of the United States, the USSR, Great Britain, and France. Recognition of Mexico's international standing came with the election of Jaime Torres Bodet as secretary-general of the United Nations. Torres Bodet served in this powerful position and was instrumental in the creation of the United Nations Education, Scientific, and Cultural Organization (UNESCO) that focused on the world's children and young people. This international organization could not prevent the Cold War when the two power blocs led by the United States and the Soviet Union emerged. Mexico, although aligned generally with its northern neighbor, did not acquiesce in the all-or-nothing red scare position of the United States. Therefore, Mexico became a scene of a good deal of intrigue between agents of the two blocs.

"Teacher, tell rural people that victory is in the harvest." The growth of the population and the demands of World War II together moved the national government toward a new emphasis on production in both the city and the countryside. Hoover Institution Political Poster Database, MX 54

Mexico as a nation witnessed changing attitudes toward life among some of its population, especially those who benefited from the bracero program in the United States. The program resulted in Mexicans, even those in subsistence agricultural regions, moving directly into the cash economy because of the remittances received from the braceros abroad.

The braceros returned with changed ideas. Although they did not adopt U.S. social or political practices, they took on their host country's ideas about consumption, material goods, and definitions of the good life, with a notable enthusiasm for home appliances.

President Miguel Alemán, who took office in 1946, represented the new generation and brought into his government other men like himself. These new men were called "pups" because of their youth. The new president was the son of a revolutionary general and governor of Veracruz who had been murdered when he supported the Escobar Rebellion against the Calles regime in 1929. Alemán, a civilian, college graduate, and city person, came to the office determined to create a framework in which the revolutionary traditions could function in a way that reflected the realities of the urban nation. He surrounded himself with individuals of similar background and like-minded politics.

More than 70 percent of his administration were college graduates, one-third of them lawyers.[2] They represented the first technocratic generation, which served as the basis for a new type of politician. Ramón Beteta, who became the first cabinet member with a college degree in economics (earned at the University of Texas), exemplified this group. His goals found expression in programs to sponsor industrialization and development. In practice, he attempted to achieve industrialization through a program of "import substitution industrialization." This method of development rested on the theory first argued by the Argentine economist Raúl Prebisch, who held that a country should produce those goods that it imported because those clearly had a market. The existence of the market solved the consumption side to development and drove production. In Mexico, this led to government support for the production of appliances and textiles—all bearing the trademark "Hecho en México" (Made in Mexico). This approach renewed the revolutionary party's concern with consumption, which had previously motivated regulations on rents and food prices.

As much as the program focused on domestic control of the economy, the most widely accepted expression of the new project came in the opening of the first Sears store in Mexico City. The Sears corporation drew on surveys of Mexican responses to radio and other media during World War II to shape its advertising campaign, and the leaders of the Sears international program in Latin America insisted the store should be placed in the hands of Mexican managers as quickly as they were trained in Chicago and had gained experience. Moreover, Sears agreed to stock appliances and textiles with the "Made in Mexico" label. The evening before the grand opening, the archbishop came to bless the store, sprinkling holy water on many of the products. The opening of Sears on February 27 proved to be one of the sensation events of 1947. Sears was instantly a success—more than 120,000 people came to the store the first day. Faced with such large crowds, the management distributed tickets so that everyone had a chance to shop. Sales on opening day totaled $600,000 and continued at that rate for weeks afterward. Eventually, Sears opened fifty-five stores across the republic.[3]

Using cash saved during the war, Mexicans in the capital city also bought apartments and homes. Revealing the class of the new owners, these houses were constructed without the small room used by maids or other domestic servants. These new bungalow homes with three bedrooms clearly targeted the middle sections of society. The middle-class desire for either a house or a condominium reflected new expectations of urban people about property ownership. Oddly, this attitude coincided with the popularity of the board game based on Monopoly in the United States, called "Turista Nacional," which had street names based on those in the national capital.

The Alemán government launched major construction projects that had multiple effects on the economy. Along with paved highways, this administration focused on new buildings, including the beautiful university city on the southern side of the capital, to unite the institutions and colleges of the National Autonomous University (UNAM), which had been dispersed across the capital city. Juan O'Gorman designed a striking library for the center of the new UNAM campus, with windowless walls covered with a mosaic of pre-Columbian images. Critics joked that the wonderful building had everything but books. The government commissioned many other official buildings across the city, and private architects undertook other projects with concrete as the basic construction material.

Besides the focus on the national capital, the president sponsored the development of the beach resort city Acapulco. His efforts included building a paved road to the Pacific coast, pressing the legal system to approve the dispossession of landholders in the area, and giving assurances of government assistance to contractors. Once the paved airstrip, improved port, and major hotels had been built, the president himself spent a good deal of time there and generally invited the stars of Hollywood, like Johnny Weissmuller, star of the Tarzan series, and political leaders to join him. Widespread tourism, including cruise ships from San Francisco and Los Angeles, followed.

The rush to construction of buildings and highways opened profitable economic opportunities and, in some cases, resulted in various forms of official and unofficial corruption, such as information leaks on building locations, use of substandard materials, bribes of housing officials, and many others. The flurry of construction provided building and service employment and generally led to an era of prosperity in cities and resorts.

In the midst of this extravaganza of construction, a steady flow of workers continued to the United States under the terms of the bracero law. These approved guest workers made a substantial contribution to the flourishing U.S. agriculture, especially in the Pacific States and Texas. The workers regularly sent money to their families, where their remittances had substantial effects, especially in terms of the construction of new permanent homes. The workers also returned with many goods purchased in the United States, ranging from pickup trucks to sporting equipment to electronic appliances.

The national rage for consumption of goods and the middle-class lifestyle soon prompted critics to produce satires of the new Mexicans of the middle sectors. Cartoonists in particular offered parodies of the clashing class views of individuals and families changing from campesino workers, revolutionary veterans, and returning braceros into bourgeois families in the new suburbs or in the new multifamily condominium buildings. The most popular of these cartoons was Gabriel Vargas's *La Familia Burrón*. Created in 1948, it continued to be the nation's most popular comic strip through the 1950s and 1960s. The Burrón family featured the wife, Borola, who had married down from a rich to a poor, working-class family, and the husband, Don Regis, a barber, who struggles to make ends meet. The family captures the overlapping modern and traditional cultures of the time, such as when Don Regis wakes up in the middle of the night with heart pains and his wife wants to rush him to doctor—by which she means finding a street vendor who sells amulets against heart attacks. The family's dysfunctional relationships brings to mind the American television show *The Simpsons*.

The works of the popular cartoonist Abel Quezada offered sarcastic images of the newly rich, especially corrupt business and political leaders, represented by diamond rings in their noses. His drawings also included celebrities such as the movie and professional wrestling star El Santo. Cartoon portrayals aside, the economy continued to grow.

The national growth rate of about 6 percent provided a tremendous sense of confidence that inspired various entrepreneurial efforts.[4] No better example of these entrepreneurial dreams exists than the effort to create Mexican Major League Baseball. The ambitious goal of Jorge Pascual and his five wealthy brothers was to challenge the major leagues in the United States. In 1946, the brothers organized their league and used their checkbooks to tempt major leaguers from the United States. None of the established stars came to Mexico, but the Pascuals successfully enticed more than a dozen big leaguers, including Sal Maglie and Mickey Owen, for what was called in the United States the "Mexican Hayride." The brothers also sought out players from the U.S. Negro Leagues and signed a number of outstanding African American players to their teams. The episode for most of the players lasted only about five months before they began seeking reinstatement in the United States. Although it did not take off, the project demonstrated the entrepreneurial thinking of businessmen who recognized the market for sports entertainment with baseball and soccer teams across the country.

Baseball was clearly an urban game, and Mexico had become an urban nation. The capital, along with the other large cities, took on a different tone characterized in some ways by the rise to prominence of a new age-group. As part of the developed world trend, teenagers became a recognized segment of the city population. Some of them appeared dangerous because of their association with gangs and crime, which led to widespread discussion of juvenile delinquency. The appearance of these individuals in movies made them all the more threatening. In Mexico as in the United States, James Dean in the title role of *Rebel without a Cause* became the archetype of restless teens. For Mexico especially, director Luis Buñuel filmed the classic urban teenage movie *Los Olvidados* (*The Forgotten*) about street gangs with all the alienation and violence of the bitter urbanism of the capital.

Nearly as widespread as these movies was the popular music that represented the drudgery and hopelessness of the lives of the poor. Typical of these songs were lyrics that referred to the overcrowded slums that, after the movies of the 1950s, were referred to as the *quinto patio*—the way back patio of tenement buildings. Despite the president's construction programs, the center of the capital city had an abandoned, slumlike character. Workers, faced with commutes to jobs, found the poor transportation system created a daytime nightmare. The most important change for the city came with the selection of a new mayor.

The capital became Ernesto Uruchurtu's obsession. As the new mayor, he reorganized the bus service in the city, largely by threatening to crack the heads of the bus drivers and their unions. He also launched a program to beautify the city through urban renewal and the creation of green spaces, both parks and gardens. He, like so many officials before and after, battled the ubiquitous street peddlers, attempting to facilitate the flow of both motorized and pedestrian traffic. As he went about the business of renewing run-down sections of town and planting gladiolas in parks and around monuments, he also initiated a moralizing campaign aimed at prostitution and crime, particularly theft and sale of stolen or misrepresented goods, and corruption. Uruchurtu's campaign in the capital city to some extent overshadowed national development programs, as Mexico became a megacity and a major tourist attraction.

The idea that tourism was the smokeless industry appealed greatly to both government administrators and private entrepreneurs who began to push for air travel as well as automobile visits to Mexico. PEMEX, the national petroleum industry, opened an office of tourism that published free pamphlets on attractions, roads, hotels, and other services in order to promote automobile tourism to ancient ruins, beautiful beaches, colonial cities, and the national capital. This campaign had a great success.

National programs moved forward as well, particularly under the direction of President Adolfo López Mateos (1958–64), who, at only forty-seven years old, brought a youthful vigor to his presidency. Widely considered to come from the same model as U.S. president John F. Kennedy and his highly visible wife, Jackie, López Mateos and his wife, Eva Samano, appeared regularly, creating ample photo opportunities of the handsome couple. Moreover, he was the first president whose election included the votes of women. After obtaining the right to vote in 1953, they cast ballots in large numbers in their first presidential election.

Women's suffrage represented a long struggle on the part of women, who worked to obtain their rightful participation in politics throughout the 1920s. President Cárdenas had intimated that he intended to amend the constitution for female suffrage, but he backed away from this commitment after the expropriation of the oil industry because he feared the issue would divide the country at the moment it needed unity to face foreign oil companies. After World War II, with a victory against the Nazi and Fascist regimes, justice and equity for all, including women, became a major program. Finally, this resulted in the 1953 amendment to the constitution.

López Mateos modeled his administration on that of Lázaro Cárdenas. The parallels between the two are striking, particularly in three areas: López Mateos reinvigorated the agrarian redistribution program to provide more land (some 30 million acres, especially in the tropical south) to rural Mexicans than any president other Cárdenas.[5] Like his predecessor, who nationalized the principal energy industry in 1938 by taking national control of oil production, López Mateos in 1962 replaced U.S. and Canadian companies with national control over the critical energy industry, electricity. Moreover, the president, like his

The National Petroleum Corporation (PEMEX) was created as a result of the 1938 expropriation of the foreign oil companies by the national government. One campaign to increase gas and oil consumption promoted automobile tourism throughout the country through the distribution of the monthly PEMEX Travel Bulletin; this issue promotes the Chichimec route. Private collection mentor, initiated a major educational program, in which his government provided both new schools and free textbooks. The Ministry of Education under Jaime Torres Bodet provided materials for prefabricated school buildings, and communities supplied the land and the labor. The free and compulsory textbooks immediately resulted in criticism from both the right and the left, as both the church and the radicals opposed the official history provided by the textbook authors, but the standardized textbook program continued and became a major source of the national culture.

The youthful, handsome López Mateos, in the fashion of Cárdenas, created a populist program that tied his government to popular culture. Noteworthy was the government's purchase of the movie industry, which had been subject to a good deal of supervision from Hollywood studios. Regulation of the movies resulted in federal control of theater ticket prices to ensure that this popular entertainment would be essentially available to all Mexicans. The production of films aimed at recapturing the popularity and screen magic of the earlier golden age.

Moreover, the president followed the cardenista model in moving against unofficial labor and political movements. Despite his support for low-cost housing for workers in the capital city and major health programs against tuberculosis, polio, and malaria, his responsible reform program did not include tolerance for unofficial strikes. He used troops, in the most dramatic moment, to break the railroad workers' strike of 1959 with the arrest of major railroad union leaders, especially Demetrio Vallejo, and to manipulate the powerful teachers union. His approach was adopted by his successor, Gustavo Díaz Ordaz, who intervened to break up a doctors' strike in 1964 and 1965.

López Mateos and Diaz Ordaz adopted a policy of support for the Cuban Revolution of Fidel Castro, up to the point at which Castro invited the USSR to build missile sites on the island. Then the Mexican leaders opposed the Soviet militarization because it could easily lead to nuclear war. At the same time, the leaders of the official party in Mexico, even though they had genuine respect for Fidel and offered continuing support to his revolutionary social and economic reforms, did not intend to allow Castro-like political groups to threaten their authority in Mexico. For the most part, the government leaders relied on the ambiguous law against social dissolution that allowed for arrests, clandestine imprisonment, and even, in some cases, death, without any accounting to relatives or the public.

Mexico's world stature grew after 1958 with the nation's selection to host the 1968 Olympic Games.[6] The decade between the end of the

López Mateos administration and the Olympics witnessed a widening gap within the nation between the incomes of the rich and poor, but more significantly between the growing population (increasing at a stunning 4.5 percent per year)[7] and the government's inability to provide social services to a people more than half of whom were under eighteen years old. Another widening break existed between right and left, both increasingly dissatisfied with the official party and the existing government. The unexpected development during this decade was the conversion of the youth culture (the rebels without a cause) of the first years after World War II into a counterculture, more political engaged and more cosmopolitan in outlook.

The student movement, centered in the capital city in the National Autonomous University (UNAM) and the National Polytechnic University, was run by students increasingly disenchanted with the official party and the national government. Mexico's selection to host the Olympic Games epitomized what many student associations found objectionable about the regime. These groups were similar to student organizations in the United States that opposed the space program. The students emphasized the growing number of Mexicans living in poverty and insisted available funds should go to a program to alleviate both economic and social inequities. Government officials and many other Mexicans took great pride in the opportunity to stage the Olympics and demonstrate grandeur of both the nation and its people. These administrators intended that no one disturb the national image that would be broadcast, in color for the first time, on international television.

The opposing views of government responsibility clashed in the summer of 1968, in ways that reflected the international university student movements of that year, which included strikes and demonstrations in Paris, Warsaw, Santiago, Tokyo, London, and, above all, Chicago and Washington, D.C. At the same time, the university activists challenged specific Mexican issues. An unrelated student issue resulted in fights between student gangs and demonstrators at the UNAM, and the national executive and his cabinet decided to authorize the use of the military to end the violence before it disrupted the general peace in the city, just prior to the Olympics. Sending soldiers or police onto the campus violated the autonomy of the university and immediately mobilized the university against the government.

Students created a leadership committee, with members from various organizations and campuses. Following the best revolutionary tactics, they rotated the persons in charge on a daily basis, so no one or two persons could be arrested and disrupt their activities. The student leaders planned silent, nonviolent demonstrations that would disrupt traffic, business, and government in the capital. They also wanted to educate the city's residents with their political views and goals by sending groups of students to perform street theater. They wrote a list of demands that they broadcast on handbills and campus radio and wanted to present to the president in person:

Freedom for the political prisoners
Freedom for the imprisoned students
Delimitation of responsibilities
Dissolution of the Riot Police
Repeal the anti-subversion law
Indemnify the families of the dead and injured...[8]

These resolutions ranged from restoring and respecting the autonomy of the universities, to the shifting of national funds from Olympic construction projects to public housing, to the release of Demetrio Vallejo, the leader of the railroad strikers in 1958–1959, who was still in prison. The student movement soon exceeded a hundred thousand in number.[9]

The coordinating committee that directed the student activities had an explicit nonconfrontational policy. This was made patently evident when the committee called for a major demonstration at the Plaza of Three Cultures, or Tlatelolco. Committee members did not call for a march on the Zócalo, the main plaza in front of the presidential offices; rather, they arranged for their demonstration in a less provocative location. They intended to have a succession of speakers and demand again that the president receive their petition. On October 12, 1968, the organizers saw a crowd of some 5,000 demonstrators in the plaza, and their presentations began in an orderly way. Suddenly the students heard the sound of approaching helicopters and, shortly afterward, bursts of gunfire into the crowd. The students panicked and tried to rush from the plaza; meanwhile, military and paramilitary troops continued to fire on them and to take prisoners. Within a matter of minutes the demonstration ended, the plaza littered with shoes, other personal items, and some bodies a mute testimony to official, planned military repression.

October 2 stands as a day of infamy. Many aspects of the tragedy remain matters of debate. What can be said with certainty is that President Gustavo Díaz Ordaz, his secretary of the interior (whose duties included domestic security), Luis Echeverría, and the chief of staff of the military had several meetings to discuss ways to prevent any social disturbances, especially student demonstrations similar to those in the United States and other countries, that might threaten the hosting of the Olympic Games. The men agreed to crash the young people with violence and arrest. Official and unofficial investigations have attempted to fix the blame for giving the order to kill the students. Recently, reports from secret agencies pointed to Echeverría, who was placed under house arrest, but the courts dismissed the charges. Other evidence suggests that the final decision came from the commanding officer at the meeting, partly in reaction to the hemming and hawing on the part of the president, who seemed to hint he wanted it done without explicitly saying so. This kind of effort to achieve deniability characterized other leaders at the time, such as disgraced President Richard Nixon in the United States.

Some aspects of the massacre will never be exactly known. How many students and other demonstrators did the army and the paramilitary murder? How many demonstrators disappeared into prison and detention camps, never to reappear? Even without answers to these questions, the indelible effects of these tragic events on the nation and the culture have become increasingly apparent.

Luis Echeverría, selected president in 1970, attempted to escape blame for the Tlatelolco events by promoting a populist regime, reminiscent of the Cárdenas years. He eased into the office in the wake of Mexico's successful hosting of the World Cup in 1970, which had turned popular attention to soccer as the Brazilian team won its third World Cup championship, led by the brilliant Pele. Despite the distraction, Echeverría soon found himself confronted by a second clash between paramilitary units and student demonstrators, the Corpus Christi violence of 1971. Nevertheless, Echeverría initiated a vigorous campaign to appeal to young Mexicans by slightly opening the political system, lowering the voting age, proposing reforms in the electoral system, and revising the representation system in Congress.

More expression of his populist intensions came with the introduction of the guayabera dress code. Often called the Yucatán wedding shirt, the guayabera hung loose, was worn untucked, and was designed for tropical climates. Echeverría chose it as the Mexican equivalent of the Mao jacket and the Castro fatigues, another fashion rejection of the formal suits and ties of European and U.S. leaders. He appealed to local sentiments when he traveled across the country, insisting on regional, semifolkloric music to introduce him. So, for example, when he went to Michoacán, a band played "Qué lindo es Michoacán" (How Beautiful Is Michoacán), in Sonora: "Sonora querida" (I Love Sonora), in Veracruz, "El Siquisirí"; and in Chiapas, "El rascapetate."[10]

The president also tried, as part of his populist effort, to be identified with the celebrities of the left and youth. Thus he attended the celebration when David Alfaro Siqueiros, one of the trio of famous muralists that also included Diego Rivera and José Clemente Orozco, completed the world's largest mural, *The March of Humanity*. Through twelve panels, the artist fused his leftist views of international progress with of a narrative of Mexican origins. Even though the mural attacked the political rhetoric that revolutionary ideals still guided the national regime, the inauguration, with the president in attendance, occurred at the specifically designed Polyforum in Mexico City in December 1971.

Echeverría's populist efforts extended to the promotion of the national handicraft industry through a national marketing agency, called FONART, which paid higher prices to the artisans. His administration moved directly into the economy, creating parastate agencies to provide entrepreneurial leadership, direct production, and distribute goods and services. When he took office, the government had owned PEMEX, the railroads, and electricity; when he left office, the government owned 1,155 companies. This program, among others, increased the national debt from $4.2 billion to $20 billion over his six-year term, but few noticed because booming oil sales created additional government income.

Echeverría's populist programs paid special attention to individuals and families, through public works programs, especially road building and rural electrification, and health care campaigns, relying heavily on the mass media of radio, television, and cinema to promote his administration. His wife, María Esther Zuno, took the lead in popularizing slogans urging women to choose how many children to have, and for parents not to have more children than they could feed and educate. Still, population growth remained at a staggering level, above 4 percent per year, and a majority of Mexicans remained younger than eighteen years old.[11]

As the population increased and the economic situation declined, Mexicans witnessed a growing number of armed challenges to the regime.[12] In the countryside, several outbreaks of rural guerrillas resulted, especially the Lucio Cabañas campaign in Guerrero. Of even more concern were urban guerrilla attacks, with kidnappings and bank robberies in cities such as Guadalajara and Monterrey. Taking hostages became, a feature of urban guerilla attacks throughout the hemisphere; victims included U.S. and British consuls, government officials, and the president's father-in-law, Guadalupe Zuno Hernández. Echeverría and his successors reacted with firmness to these challenges while they attempted to maintain their revolutionary reputations. Even for those who did not take up arms against the president, cynical doubt existed about Echevarría's programs and sarcastic commentary about the repose of the nation's wealthy citizens flourished. In a 1974 edition of the popular comic strip *La Familia Burrón*, the extremely rich Aunt Cristela moved to Paris to escape Echeverría's attacks on multimillionaires.[13]

In the midst of the Cold War, the spread of Castro-like rebellions, and the response of military leaders who seized power and carried out wars of arrest, torture, and murder of radicals and suspected radicals in the hemisphere, Echeverría sought to become a leader of those nations that were not aligned with the United States or the USSR, and who opposed the military dictatorships. He sought to become the secretary-general of the United Nations, or some similar international body. He founded the Tri-continental University as a political base. His efforts proved unsuccessful, in part because hints began to appear that the official party and his regime had followed policies that seemed to have undercut national prosperity and populist reforms.

Echeverría's administration had a Janus-like character, with one face turned toward the populist program aimed at the left with programs for youths, women, and workers, especially in the countryside, and the other face turned toward the right, with entrenched officials committed to consolidation of authority by elimination of challengers. Echeverría either ordered or allowed the use of security forces to move against both urban and rural guerrillas, the imposition of so-called *charro* or cowboy union leaders tied to the government, and the breaking of any serious labor challenges to his administration. Labor secretary Fidel Velázquez played principal in the politics of suppression.

Most dramatic was the struggle between government labor officials and electrical workers. After losing their fight for control of the union, more than 100,000 electrical workers and supporters organized a strike at the Federal Electrical Commission on July 16, 1976. The government officials used army units and hired thugs to halt the demonstration as they occupied the power plants and took into custody hundreds of strikers, who were then interned in San Luis Potosí.

Parallel to the politics of the official party and president, business leaders, especially in the north and west, sought ways to protect themselves against government policies (both the Echeverría agrarian programs that recognized land invasions and peso devaluations). A number of these businessmen moved into the Partido de Acción Nacional (PAN), where their views in many ways contradicted the party's Catholic social action mentality. Vatican II, a meeting from 1962 to 1965 of all bishops of the church, had focused on the needs of people, changed the Mass from Latin to local languages, and inspired priests to work for social reforms to eliminate poverty. The PAN had quickly taken on social work projects. Shortly afterward in 1975, business interests won control of the party, eliminated the social orientation, and focused on what they regarded as more entrepreneurial programs. They also pushed the party to challenge the Institutional Revolutionary Party (PRI) in local and state elections. These policies soon resulted in a growing number of PAN elected officials.

Echeverría's presidency ended as it began, with a high tide of opposition to the regime, made worse by world conditions, including oil price declines and general economic downturns that hurt Mexico. In this situation, Mexicans had to endure inflation that forced two devaluations of the peso in 1976 from 12.50 to 30 pesos to the U.S. dollar.

José López Portillo, the next president, chose to see only positive economic indicators provided by new oil strikes, especially off the Gulf Coast, as he ignored the warning signs implicit in Echevarría's devaluation of the peso. For the first three years of his term, the optimistic view held, even though the signs of deep problems grew more strident in the countryside and the need for food imports increased. Then the economy began to collapse, and throughout the remainder of his administration economic difficulties harried the president. The downturned economy eroded the lifestyle of the middle sectors and pushed the poor into the cities or across the border in search of work. López Portillo steadfastly declared he would not allow another devaluation; he insisted he was, in his words, "defending the peso, like a dog defends its bone."[14]

His best intentions aside, he found Mexico's economic choices were severely limited because of the huge international debt the government had accumulated based on its petroleum dreams. The economic tailspin forced dramatic actions. López Portillo tried to capture popular imagination, as had Cárdenas and López Mateos, by asserting national control over a sector of the economy. While his predecessors garnered great support after the nationalization of the petroleum and electrical industries, López Portillo received nothing but blame and censure when he nationalized the banking system. Shortly before he left office, he added to the grave situation by devaluing the peso once again to sixty-nine pesos to the dollar. This devaluation, coupled with the nationalizing the banking system and freezing the conversion of accounts into dollars, had a devastating effect on the economy. A complete change of lifestyle for the general public followed.[15]

CHAPTER EIGHT

Contemporary Mexico

When President José López Portillo devalued the peso yet again in 1982, he created a national situation in which Mexicans had to change their everyday lives and how they prepared for the future. From the vantage point of customary activities, consumer practices, and social behavior that had resulted over the years as a result of the revolutionary political, educational, health, and economic programs, people had to adopt new habits. The response to the 1982 devaluation ended the revolution's impact on daily life by changing the national culture. Mexicans learned that the national government that had been essential in revolutionary programs involving land, labor, education, health, housing, food prices, and restrictions on foreigners no longer functioned in these areas. Devaluation, unemployment, spiraling international debts, zooming inflation, and escalating costs of living had devastating effects on the society. The collateral damage of devaluation could be seen most clearly in two developments: the steady decline of the purchasing power of wages, and the increase in the informal economy as a response to the desperate search to earn a living. Said more simply, trying to save money no longer made sense, and crime (including the trade in illegal drugs) offered a steady income.[1]

The values associated with saving money for the family's education, new homes, or old age disappeared with frozen bank accounts and the collapsing value of the peso. A circus of consumer buying resulted, in which people tried to spend the money they had before its value disappeared. They tried to buy appliances, real estate, or durable goods that would retain their value. At the same time, these purchases of cars, homes, appliances, and even fashionable clothes attracted the attention of the burgeoning number of criminals whose activities increased carjackings and home break-ins and soon escalated to kidnappings.

These crimes did not overshadow revelations of government corruption during the López Portillo administration. President Miguel de la Madrid (1982–88) initiated his presidency committed to identifying and punishing corrupt officials. His two most sensational convictions came against López Portillo officials: Jorge Díaz Serrano, the onetime director of PEMEX, the government petroleum corporation; and Arturo Durazo, the police chief of the Federal District. De la Madrid's government successfully prosecuted Díaz Serrano for embezzling an amount equal to $43 million, but bringing Durazo to justice proved more difficult. Popularly known as "El Negro Durazo," the police chief fled the country and managed to avoid extradition until 1986. When he was finally placed on trial, the record of his murders, corruption, extravagance, and self-indulgence staggered popular imagination. His salary of sixty-five dollars a week could not explain his palatial compound in Mexico City complete with a replica of the New York disco Studio 54, nor the beach estate at Zihuatanego, nor his mammoth self-indulgence in collecting rare automobiles, race horses, and trophy wines, but murders, narcotics, and extortion did. His activities became the subject of at least a half dozen popular songs, including the group Super Show de los Vaskez's song with a *cumbia* beat, called "Duro, Duro, Durazo" (Tough, Tough Guy Durazo).[2]

This spectacle, nevertheless, could not right the economy as the nation suffered one calamity after another. As the value of the peso continued to spiral downward, citizens could neither catch their breath nor develop coping strategies before the peso dropped again. In the midst of this stunning financial experience, the nation received a staggering blow on September 19, 1985, with an earthquake that reached over eight on the ten-point Richter scale of seismic movement. The quake caused damages across an area of more than 100 miles. It was felt in Houston, Texas (745 miles away), and Guatemala City (621 miles away), but focused on the capital city. Considered to have the equivalent force of the 1906 San Francisco event, the 1985 earthquake caused damages estimated at $4 billion; more than 400 buildings collapsed, and at least 3,000 were damaged. A minimum of 10,000 people died, and countless thousands were injured.

President de la Madrid responded in a bafflingly slow way. Because he feared the catastrophe might result in a military takeover of his government, he refused to let the army mobilize its strategic emergency program. This policy forced the stunned, injured citizens to search for, rescue, or recover bodies of those buried in rubble on their own and to deal with the dire situation without homes, food, or water. The courage lacking in the president and his advisers appeared in the ordinary citizens who quickly established community groups to meet the crisis.

One of the most devastated sections of the capital was the Plaza of Three Cultures, or Tlatelolco, where the 1968 massacre had occurred. Around the plaza, the apartment and condominium buildings that had

On September 19, 1985, shortly after 7:00 AM, an earthquake measuring at 8.1 on the Richter scale struck Mexico City. It was followed by two major aftershocks. An estimated 10,000 people died, primarily from collapsing buildings, and the national government did little to help. Photo by M. Celebi. Courtesy of the U.S. Geological Survey

been built with substandard materials collapsed and buried hundreds in the rubble. The community reacted quickly, and their efforts attracted the attention of leaders across the nation and the world. Even though the president refused to ask for help, international leaders came to Mexico with funds for assistance. These included the presidents of Brazil (José Sarney), Venezuela (Jaime Lusinchi), Spain (Felipe González), and Peru (Alan García), and the U.S. First Lady, Nancy Reagan. International tenor virtuoso Plácido Domingo, who had an aunt, uncle, and other relatives killed in one of the apartment buildings, came to Tlatelolco with aid and stayed to work with the rescue brigades. The following year, he and Colombian diva Martha Senn sang benefit concerts for the victims in San Antonio, Texas, and other international locations. Today a statue, made from the keys to apartments in the neighborhood's lost buildings, commemorates his aid to the neighborhood.[3]

The presidential lack of nerve to make decisions further undermined PRI authority with the general population and increased political opportunities for the opponents of the official party. The presidents and party leaders after Echeverría had largely ignored developments associated with the opposition, especially with the PAN, as they focused on the internal divisions within the party. A growing number of PRI members, especially the upcoming generation, wanted a more open, democratic party that recognized political experience rather than technical (especially economic) expertise. The push in this direction initially came from Echeverría, who reviewed the party's procedures and made recommendations to make it a more popular, that is, a more responsive, organization.

Echeverría's reforms had as an inspiration the earlier reform proposals by PRI party president during the years 1964–1965, Carlos Madrazo, who was the secretary of the interior. Madrazo attempted to revitalize the party by removing officials who had held positions for decades or were widely known for corrupt practices. He called for party primaries for local offices (instead of appointment of candidates by party leaders) and the institution of a Commission of Honor to review charges of electoral corruption or administrative malfeasance. Díaz Ordaz, backed by longtime party regulars such as the secretary of labor, Fidel Velázquez, who soon became known collectively as "dinos" (the dinosaurs), removed Madrazo from office, but his proposed reforms had inspired Echeverría. The democratic sector within the party continued to grow and push for more say in PRI decisions and, a decade later, became members of the Democratic Current, a group that soon abandoned the party.

Outside of politics, following the earthquake, desperate individuals sought solutions to their plight. For a growing number, immigration to the United States seemed the only alternative to crime. Alarming anti-immigrant politics in the United States made the process more difficult and increasingly dangerous. Beginning in 1993 the U.S. Border Patrol and Customs Service took a harder line against people crossing the border, arresting undocumented persons and deporting them. Some prospective immigrants sought more remote locations to cross (usually in extreme deserts) that exposed them to natural hazards. Others turned to smugglers (called coyotes) who for prices as high as $4,000 a person or more would arrange illegal entry into the United States. Coyotes, rather than face arrest themselves if things went wrong, abandoned their customers in the desert or anywhere else. Due to these two developments many more immigrants died in their attempts to cross into the United States.

Domestically, some of the desperate turned to demonstrations to pressure the government to sponsor relief programs. The peso continued its downward spiral, losing value from 26 pesos to the dollar in 1982 to 2,300 pesos to the dollar in 1987. At this point the World Bank and the

International Monetary Fund in exchange for assistance demanded the introduction of neoliberal policies, especially freezing wages, cutting government social expenses, and privatizing government agencies, such as the telephone company. These policies only had the effect of further contracting the economy.

The 1988 presidential election culminated in the political harvest of the Echeverría populist programs. The presidential competition included three candidates, who received nearly an equal number of votes. Carlos Salinas de Gotarí, who had never before run for an elected office but who had bureaucratic experience in the government and technical economic training at Harvard University, represented the PRI. By the late 1980s the PAN was dominated by business and agricultural leaders who had banded together in opposition to rural land invasions by landless people allowed by the Echeverría policies. The PAN nominated Manuel Clouthier, who promised to end electoral fraud and government corruption, while shifting economic activity to the private sector. Echeverría carried out significant changes in the political system to create an opening for greater democracy. A sector within the PRI had begun to demand these changes and additional reforms. Cuauhtémoc Cárdenas, highly visible as the successful PRI governor of Michoacán (1980–1986) and as the son of the former president, gave this group a formal structure as the Corriente Democrática.

When this Democratic Current nominated him as presidential candidate, party dinos led by Fidel Velázquez demanded his expulsion from the PRI. Cárdenas led his group out of the party and organized a reform coalition called the Frente Democrático Nacional (Democratic National Front), demanding political and economic changes. The 1988 election results revealed a virtual dead heat among the candidates until government officials reported that "se cayó el sistema" (the system had crashed). Once technicians repaired the IBM AS/400 vote-counting system, the computer declared Salinas the winner. A wave of outrage washed across the republic against what nearly everyone believed was electoral fraud, whether they supported Clouthier or Cárdenas. "Se cayó el sistema" became a reference not to the computer but to the PRI-run government. Widespread demands mounted for electoral reforms.[4]

Salinas's presidential victory in 1988 can be compared to the Alemán election in 1946 for its introduction of a new generation of technocrats into major government offices. He recruited his college-trained, civilian administrators from his network of acquaintances from the national law school and the national school of economics. More than 94 percent of his appointments held college degrees, and of these only one in three was a lawyer. Salinas remains the only president to ever graduate from the National University (UNAM). His career path to the presidency through financial agencies rather than elected offices, followed by his successor, Miguel de la Madrid, established a pattern continued until the monumental election of 2000. Among the junior members of this group of technocrats, they, unlike the president, did their undergraduate training at private rather than public universities. Besides degrees in economics, they shared another characteristic: graduate training in this discipline in the United States, especially at either Harvard or Yale University.

The new president also vigorously promoted a North American trade zone with the United States and Canada with the idea that increased trade, improved jobs, and expanded investment would follow. Questions arose in all three countries, but many politicians argued that the formation of the European Union created a trading bloc that required some sort of North American common market to compete. Despite strong opposition in all three nations, the presidents signed the North American Free Trade Agreement (NAFTA). It proved a costly political decision.

Salinas had a plan for his government inspired by Poland's Solidarity movement led by Lech Wałęsa that focused on community reforms outside of government agencies; his own 1978 Ph.D. dissertation on reform policies done at Harvard University's Kennedy School and published in 1980 as *Production and Political Participation in the Countryside* that proposed working outside the usual bureaucracies to make government assistance more efficient; and the book *Modernization Proposals for the Agricultural and Livestock Industry*, published in 1975 by the Business Coordinating Council, that called for constitutional changes, repeated the plan to eliminate bureaucratic procedures that led to money and initiative being siphoned off. Generally, Salinas intended to create a process that provided finances to respond to community needs and to deliver the funds directly to community groups, bypassing the bureaucracy that siphoned off money through overhead and corruption. He wanted to bring the laws into accord with practices that resulted from the crisis of 1982. A number of these legal changes required constitutional amendments that the Congress with a majority of dinos would not address. At this point, the earlier Echeverría congressional changes came into play, as President Salinas backed the midterm election of representatives open to daring changes in the constitution. A series of amendments followed that stunned citizens and observers.

The Salinas reforms faced major opposition from those committed to the revolutionary programs as earlier defined, longtime party regulars, especially the dinos, leftists within and outside the party committed to either agrarian or proletarian Marxist programs, and others just suspicious of change. Salinas pushed ahead in a series of daring amendments. The most encompassing amendment changed the definition of the identity of the Mexican. Salinas replaced the idea of the mestizo, a member of the Cosmic Race and expression of the melding of ethnic diversity of the nation, by what in the United States would be called a politically correct statement of diversity. The new amendment redefined the population as having a "pluricultural composition" on an indigenous base and went on to guarantee government protections for indigenous languages and customs.

More widely seen as an indication of this change was the image used on the cover of the national textbooks distributed to all schoolchildren in grades one through twelve. The cover painting purported to show an indigenous woman as the mother of the nation, "La Patria," modeled on the image of Victoria Dorenlas, according to oral tradition the perfect example of Mexican womanhood and therefore the image of the nation. How this story developed, and even if she actually lived or was just a myth, has been lost. Jorge González Camarena, went to Tlaxco, Tlaxcala, where supposedly she had lived and found no record of her, although many residents claimed their grandparents had known her. He saw the statue to her in the town and used it as a model for his painting. The image served as the cover since the publication of the first books in 1960 until 1972, when it was replaced because of charges that it did not accurately depict the Mexican people. Salinas reinstated the portrait in line with his redefinition of the people as part of his program to give new vitality to previous revolutionary programs.[5]

More controversial within the nation and among international Mexico observers was the revision of the constitutional amendment, Article 27, that defined agrarian reform and the *ejido* (communal land) program. The *ejido* for many defined the revolution, and Salinas on several occasions declared it a failure, responsible for rural underdevelopment and the national need to import foods, especially grains, since the 1970s. The amendment allowed the privatization of *ejidos*, thus permitting individual ownership of the property, along with the mortgaging, renting, and selling of the land—all previously illegal for the communal owners.

The outrage expressed against the Salinas constitutional changes increased as the president also revised the seventy-five-year-old anticlerical provisions of the constitution that prevented church ownership of property, church-operated schools, religious public celebrations without civil approval, and foreign priests. The president welcomed Pope John Paul II to Mexico and, after a break of 130 years, established diplomatic relations with the Vatican.

Beyond the constitution, Salinas created a neoliberal regime as he abandoned the government's entrepreneurial role, pushed to extreme levels by Echeverría with the creation of more than 1,000 parastate industries. Although Salinas did not dare tamper with PEMEX, he sold to private individuals roughly 1,000 of these government enterprises, most dramatically the national banks, Banco Nacional de México (BANAMEX) and Banco de Comercio (BANCOMER), and the national telecommunications industry, Teléfonos de México (TELMEX).

The president's version of Poland's Solidarity movement, called the Programa Nacional de Solidaridad (PRONASOL; National Program of Solidarity), successfully funded numerous community programs requested and managed by local groups outside the structure of the bureaucracy. The program recognized and financed the kind of self-help neighborhood organizations that formed in the wake of the 1985 earthquake. The projects included cooperative marketing groups, local bridges, community road improvements, new schools, and town electricity. Justifiably proud of these programs, Salinas saw them as major achievements, but PRONASOL was abruptly overshadowed on January 1, 1994.

The 1988 Salinas election had created a ticking time bomb for PRI's political authority. The rampant voting irregularities and outright fraud had reached such levels that the party's survival depended on the implementation of genuine election guarantees. Salinas created the independent Federal Electoral Institute (Instituto Federal Electoral or IFE) in 1990 as a major step toward just such guarantees. With it came the growing popular conviction that the PRI would soon be defeated in a presidential contest. The first test came in the 1994 election, but this campaign was disrupted by three abrupt developments.

First came the rebellion of the Zapatista Army of National Liberation (EZLN) with its cadres in ski masks and their bizarre commander, self-styled as Subcomandante Marcos, armed with a laptop computer. The EZLN demanded respect for indigenous peoples, programs to ameliorate local poverty, and an end to the endorsement of wage compression that rebels and many others believed would result from the North American Free Trade Agreement. Although the EZLN is most widely known for its demands to protect and develop the rights of indigenous peoples, the organization made clear statements about the rights of all Mexican women. In its "Women's Revolutionary Law," of January 8, 1994, it outlined female entitlements:

> Women, regardless of their race, creed, color or political affiliation, have the right to participate in the revolutionary struggle in any way that their desire and capacity determine.
> Women have the right to work and receive a fair salary.
> Women have the right to decide the number of children they have and care for.
> Women have the right to participate in the matters of the community and have charge if they are free and democratically elected.
> Women and their children have the right to Primary Attention in their health and nutrition.
> Women have the right to an education.
> Women have the right to choose their partner and are not obliged to enter into marriage.
> Women have the right to be free of violence from both relatives and strangers.[6]

The call for reforms reflected the equity within the EZLN, where men and women shared equally the leadership and responsibilities of the group. Moreover, it demonstrated the growing concern of women across the nation about the civil marriage ceremony (the Epistle of Melchor Ocampo), statements of the wife's subordinate position to the husband being discussed in congress, and the widespread calls for efforts to reduce domestic violence against women.

The EZLN declared revolution on January 1, 1994, in Chiapas, the nation's poorest state, with the largest indigenous population. The Zapatistas quickly captured several towns, including San Cristóbal de Las Casas, in the highlands. Federal troops swept into the region. Only an armistice prevented a bloodbath. Bishop Samuel Ruiz, known for his efforts to assist the indigenous communities in Chiapas, organized negotiations that made clear that the indigenous organizations that grew from the First National Congress of Indigenous Peoples in 1975, based on cultural groups, had not been merely going through the motions but in fact intended to achieve major, genuine reforms for Indians. The EZLN rebellion put politicians on notice that indigenous Mexicans would no longer accept marginal status but intended to claim a more equitable life.

The rebellion was immediately followed by revelations about corruption and murders directed by the president's family and the assassination of the PRI's presidential candidate, Luis Donaldo Colosio, in Tijuana, Baja California del Norte, in March 1994. This threatening political environment fostered timidity about change that helped the PRI reach victory with its substitute candidate for president, Ernesto Zedillo.

Nevertheless, Zedillo's term seemed only to provide a framework for the ghastly revelations about the levels of embezzlement, intimidation, and murder reached by former president Salinas's brother, Raúl, and other immediate family members. The murder of José Francisco Ruiz Massieu led to Raúl's incarceration and then further revelations about both Ruiz Massieu's family ties to drug cartels and corruption schemes that ended in the suicide of Mario Ruiz Massieu in New Jersey, where he was avoiding extradition. Raúl, it was soon revealed, had accumulated a fortune reaching the hundreds of millions of dollars by charging a 10 percent fee for access to his political influence. The climax came in a sensational public trial in which he was found guilty. In a nation without a death sentence, he received a fifty-year sentence (later reduced nearly by half on appeal).[7]

The Salinas scandal would not go away, and it soon undercut the former president's reputation. He fled into exile, eventually settling in Ireland, while suspicions about his personal involvement in the corruption rackets swirled about and the nation enjoyed the grim humor that became known as Salinasmania. On street corners in the capital and other cities, vendors sold figures and T-shirts depicting the former president as a rat, a *chupacabra*, or a prisoner with fists full of dollars available . Cartoonists caricatured his image, and street singers lampooned his administration. He became a laughingstock.

As his predecessor's legacy was destroyed, President Zedillo pushed to negotiate an end to the Zapatista rebellion. These efforts ended in the San Andrés Accords of February 1996, which attempted to define indigenous rights and culture. Basic provisions recognized indigenous diversity and extended to indigenous pueblos control over local natural resources of land, timber, and water, public expenditures, and local political procedures. The public optimism that followed the announcement of the accords dissipated quickly as the government could not deliver the implementation legislation to realize the agreement.

The continuation of the Zapatista movement, the stunning revelations of the Salinas era crime and corruption, and the rising tide of immigration to the United States created the context for a growing

Revelations of Carlos Salinas de Gotari's corruption and the crimes, including murder, of his brother Raúl and other associates sparked the production of satirical images, t-shirts, songs, toys, and songs, together called "Salinasmania." This is the catalog for the Salinas museum, which was created in the bathroom of a private apartment. Smart Art Press

number of opposition political victories over the PRI at both the local and state levels. Particularly in the north, state and local governments fell under PAN control, and in the nation's center region the Party of Democratic Revolution (PRD), the successor to the Democratic Current, won local victories, most dramatically in 1997 when Cuauhtémoc Cárdenas won the office of head of the Federal District, an office roughly equivalent to mayor of Mexico City. Governing a city with a population roughly equal to that of Canada, he proved to be an effective administrator, skillful politician, and honest official. These events set the stage for the 2000 presidential election.

Once again three candidates contended for the position. The best-known individual was Cuauhtémoc Cárdenas, who resigned his position to run on the PRD ticket. He faced the PRI choice, Francisco Labastida, and the PAN candidate, Vicente Fox. All three had previously held elected offices. Labastida also had served in two presidential cabinets, and Fox had a reputation as an outstanding business leader, based on his management of Coca-Cola first in Mexico and then throughout Latin America. For the first time, the candidates faced each other in a presidential debate on television, and voting analysts later concluded that appearances had a major impact in the choice of winner.

The campaign ended in July 2000 with a victory for PAN candidate Fox. Fox won in an election almost free of voting disruption (there were scattered incidents of voter intimidation) as the polls were monitored by more than 80,000 observers recruited and trained by civic groups to prevent corruption. Once the official announcement came that, with 42.5 percent of the ballots counted, Fox had defeated his opponents, sitting president Zedillo delivered a dignified speech that offered congratulations and promised a smooth transition to the new government.[8] Mexicans, in exuberant celebration, swept to the streets to celebrate what they believed represented a new age of democracy. The report of outside election observers concluded that the election was "a clear demonstration that great changes have taken place in Mexican society. Fox's victory buil[t] on Mexican citizens' prolonged struggle for democracy."[9] With all the flags, banners, car horns, and crowds of a World Cup championship, Mexicans rejoiced across the republic over the first defeat of the PRI candidate for president since the party's creation in 1929.

Fox brought a huge change to governmental administration. His appointment of government officials introduced a large number of people without college degrees, but with business experience. Often they came from rural backgrounds—in that capacity they represented a greater portion of the administration, 20 percent compared with 12 percent, than even the revolutionary administrations of Obregón and Calles.[10] The outpouring of celebration for the democratic victory unexpectedly previewed the dramatic increase of opportunities for citizens of lower class origins to enter the government. The revolutionary generation had closed the door to government to most upper-class individuals and provided greatest opportunities to rural, middle-class veterans, but the PAN election of 2000 threw open the doors of opportunities to lower- and working-class politicians.[11] Despite the euphoria of victory, the new administration had a short-lived honeymoon.

The new president and his party faced major problems as administrative realities appeared. Of these the most difficult for the president was the Congress, usually thought of as a rubber stamp. Controlled by the PRI, it now represented a formidable obstacle to executive programs. Midterm elections in 2003 strengthened the PRI hold on both representative bodies. The Congress stonewalled the president on as many issues as possible—providing a lesson in one of the difficulties of democratic government. The president also learned that politics, unlike his business ventures and rational choice in political science, did not always seem to make sense. He had declared during the presidential campaign that if elected he would settle the EZLN rebellion in fifteen minutes. He tried.

The president moved quickly to withdraw army troops from Chiapas, free EZLN prisoners from jail, and introduce legislation that granted indigenous community control over lands and resources proposed by the Zapatistas in Congress. Placing these efforts in the context of general indigenous difficulties, he created a new position and named the successful Otomí consultant, Xochitl Gálvez, as the director of the Comisionada Nacional para el Desarrollo de los Pueblos Indígenas (Office of Indian Affairs). The EZLN and its leader, Subcomandante Marcos, organized a long march, dubbed the "Zapatour," from Chiapas, winding through twelve states, to Mexico City to promote the legislation. Fox supported an appearance of EZLN leaders before Congress, but his own PAN and the PRI opposed it. The president prevailed, but hard-line congressmen boycotted the session, and Marcos did not appear. Rather Comandante Esther, a Maya, captured national attention with a speech calling for approval of the legislation that received national television coverage. Congress eventually approved the Indian Rights Bill, without the community autonomy guaranteed in the earlier San Andrés Accords. The EZLN refused to recognize it as the fulfillment of its promised legislation. Therefore, both the EZLN and the indigenous issue remained a troubling political concern.

The new president made some decisions that many found socially inappropriate. One year after his inauguration, Fox (who was divorced) married his onetime spokesperson, a divorcée. The new First Lady, Marta Sahagán, had no intention of playing the demure housewife of Los Pinos, the executive residence. Her sudden entrance into public life startled many traditional citizens, even though she had ample role models, from Eva Perón to Hillary Clinton. She appeared often in public, spoke her mind, and established a major charity in her own name. Critics sarcastically ignored her status as First Lady, addressing her with the familiar diminutive Martita, with echoes of a contemporary melodramatic TV soap opera *Simplemente Maria*, that soon spawned a caustic biography, *Simplemente Martita*. Her penchant for referring to herself and the president as the presidential couple soon prompted rumors that she planned to succeed her husband in the office. She later discounted these accounts. Because she was a woman of strong political opinions and social activity, despite satirical comments, she represents a tradition of First Ladies including Margarita Maza de Juárez, Carmen Romero de Díaz, and Amalia Solorzano de Cárdenas. Each played significant, if out of the public eye, roles in the administrations of their husbands.

The 2006 election built on the democratic experience of 2000 and once again featured three candidates from the PRI, PAN, and PRD. The latter party's candidate, Andrés López Obrador, mayor of Mexico City (called the head of government of the Federal District), quickly emerged as the early leader in popularity polls over the PAN choice, Felipe Calderón, and the PRI nominee, Roberto Madrazo, a distant third. A turning point in the election came with the plan for a national debate on television. López Obrador refused to participate with the other two, creating an impression with voters of a strikingly undemocratic individual. His popularity began to fall in polls.

When the Federal Election Institute announced Felipe Calderón as the winner, it was the narrowest of victories, based on only 0.58 percent more votes.[12] Madrazo gracefully accepted a second PRI defeat, but López Obredor, with an anguish born of his campaign mistakes, refused to concede. He declared that substantial election fraud had occurred at 30 percent of the polls, and that he himself was the winner. Although AMLO, as his followers styled him by using his initials, established a parallel cabinet and called on the PRD and supportive congressmen to block the inauguration, it proceeded, and Calderón took office.

Calderón's election seemed to indicate another change in the training of individuals in political life. The new president, a lawyer rather than an economist, brought other lawyers into his administration. More interesting was the number of individuals recruited to his government with backgrounds in computer science, communications, and the sciences. Perhaps these disciplines provide responses to the growing complexities of national life. The pursuit of advanced degrees abroad, in either the United States or Europe, remains constant with this generation of politicians.[13]

The political system has become increasingly democratic, but the establishment of a more responsible presidential system has not, and the office cannot resolve some major problems. One of the most severe difficulties is the growing prevalence of illegal drug trading organizations. Drug cartels on both the Atlantic and Pacific coasts of the republic have become increasingly active. No documentation exists, but innuendo and between-the-lines events make clear that some modus operandi had previously existed between the PRI and the cartels. The parameters seem to have been an agreement that if the cartels did nothing to expand drug usage in Mexico, but focused on shipments to the United States, the PRI government would only go through the motions of an antidrug campaign. This working agreement began to break down as a result of three political developments. First, the election of PAN presidents in 2000 and 2006, with their commitment to ending government corruption and connections to the crime world, led to an intensification of antidrug enforcement. The construction of a border fence between the United States and Mexico complicated drug shipments and increased pressure from the U.S. government on Mexican officials to reduce drug flows. The results include a war among the cartels, armed with weapons purchased in Texas and U.S. southwest, and government agencies of the police and army, increased murders in the border towns, and infiltration by the cartels into government agencies, usually accomplished by paying informants. In one well-publicized instance, army major Arturo González Rodríguez, in charge of President Calderón's daily agenda, was receiving $100,000 a month from a cartel (he was arrested in December, 2008).[14] The struggle will only intensify as it is not just a Mexican drug problem but, as numerous investigations of the drug-inspired violence has shown, one born of the illegal market in the United States.[15]

Another complex problem results from international migration.[16] For years, desperate individuals in Mexico and Central America have crossed into the United States, found available jobs, and sent remittance money home. The international war between terrorists and the United States, especially following the 2001 attack on New York City's World Trade Center, resulted in policies to regulate and restrict immigration.

The skyline of Mexico City only hints at the size of what is arguably the world's different than those of any other megalopolis—air pollution, shortages of water they are magnified by its size. Shutterstock

The growing antiforeign attitudes, especially in the southwestern region of the United States, became increasingly rabid with the decision of President George W. Bush to approve the construction of a fence along the border. The complex of issues involving public health, minimum-wage jobs, human rights, and deportations just scratch the surface of the growing complications between the United States, Mexico, and Central American nations. The Calderón government cannot solve the problem alone. Until the U.S. government can resolve the asymmetrical relationship between the need for security against suspected terrorists (often only a rationalization in the southwestern United States for anti-foreign attitudes, the open sale of weapons especially in Texas and Arizona, and employment fears in a difficult economy) and the appropriate tradition of welcoming immigrants and endorsing human rights, no international agreement seems possible.

For all the difficult situations that the government and the people face, in 2010 Mexican citizens can take pride in the celebration of two

largest city, with more than 22 million people. Mexico City's problems are no and public utilities, widespread crime, and traffic and human congestion—but centuries of independence and one century of revolutionary social change. Mexicans have created a society and government that is more committed to political equality, social opportunity, and ethnic diversity than at anytime in its past. The history of overcoming daunting challenges and the growth of a more equitable society gives hope for the future.

Chronology

40,000–200 BCE
Archaic Era: hunter-gatherers, domestication of maize and other crops

2000 BCE
Appearance of small villages and trade throughout Meso-America

200 BCE–200 CE
Formative Era, also called Pre-Classic Era: Olmec religious-political centers with large populations and intense agricultural production

200–900 CE
Classic Era: diversification of social-political roles; development of science, architecture, and calendar systems; widespread use of obsidian; principal centers in Tikal, Monte Albán, and Teotihuacán

900–1521 CE
Post-Classic Era: Maya culture shifts north to Chichen Itza and Tulum; Toltec culture develops with major site at Tula; Zapotec culture develops with a center at Mitla

1375
Aztecs establish their island capital at Tenochtitlán on island in Lake Texcoco and begin building their empire

1519–1821
Spanish colonial era

1519–August 13, 1521
Spanish conquest of the Aztec capital of Tenochtitlán

1521–1703
Spanish Hapsburg dynasty rules Mexico

1531
Traditional date for the appearance of the Virgin of Guadalupe

1535
Spanish crown creates the viceroyalty of New Spain

1703–1821
Spanish Bourbon dynasty rules Mexico

1713–1806
Bourbon reforms of government, economy, and society

1810–21
Mexican struggle for independence from Spain

September 16, 1810
Padre Miguel Hidalgo calls for independence

1812
Spanish and provincial delegates write the Spanish Imperial Constitution of Cádiz

September 27, 1821
Agustín Iturbide defeats Spaniards and achieves Mexican independence

July 22, 1822, to March 19, 1823
Iturbide's empire of Mexico

1824 to 1846
Antonio López de Santa Anna in and out of power

October 2, 1835
Texas Rebellion

1838–39
Pastry War with France

December 29, 1845
United States annexes Texas

May 13, 1846
United States declares war on Mexico, begins U.S.-Mexican War

February 2, 1848
Treaty of Guadalupe Hidalgo ends war between the United States and Mexico; Mexico yields half of its national territory to the United States

1855–76
Liberal Era; Benito Juárez acting and elected president, 1855–1872

1857
Liberals write their constitution with separation of church and state, equality before the law, and attacks on landholding by the church and indigenous communities

1859
Epistle of Melchor Ocampo on duties of men and women incorporated into the civil marriage ceremony

1862–67
French intervention in Mexico

May 5, 1863
Mexican victory over French troops at Puebla, commemorated as the Cinco de Mayo holiday

1863–67
Reign of French-backed emperor and empress, Maximilian and Carlotta

1876–1911
Porfirio Díaz regime; era of dramatic economic development, including railroads, mines, factories, and commercial agriculture; repressive political administration

1910–46
The Mexican Revolution; more than 2 million (about 1 in 7) Mexicans die in first decade

February 22, 1913
Assassination of revolutionary president Francisco Madero

January 1, 1915
First agrarian reform law passed

1917
Revolutionary Constitution of 1917 stressed the mestizo nature of the population and called for land reform, workers' rights, education, and public health programs

April 10, 1919
Assassination of revolutionary agrarian leader Emiliano Zapata

May 21, 1920
Assassination of revolutionary president Venustiano Carranza

1921–24
José Vasconcelos, minister of education, develops programs for rural education, murals, and photographic documentation of the culture of indigenous peoples

July 20, 1923
Assassination of revolutionary leader Pancho Villa

1923–24
De la Huerta Rebellion against the Obregón government

1926–29
Cristero Rebellion against the revolutionary government

July 17, 1928
Assassination of revolutionary president-elect Alvaro Obregón

March 18, 1938
President Cárdenas expropriates the foreign oil industry

1946–82
The Mexican Miracle: era punctuated by economic growth and urbanization, especially in Mexico City; increased number of strikes by railroad workers, doctors, and teachers

1953
Women receive the right to vote

October 2, 1968
Government ordered massacre of students at the Plaza of Tlatelolco

August 5, 1982
End of the Mexican Miracle with the devaluation of the peso by 72 percent

1988–94
Presidency of Carlos Salinas de Gotarí; series of constitutional amendments revising land programs and the definition of Mexican nationality

January 1, 1994
Signing of the North American Free Trade Agreement

January 1, 1994
Rebellion of the Zapatista Army of National Liberation (EZLN) in Chiapas

July 2, 2000
Vicente Fox wins first victory by opposing party over the revolutionary party in a presidential election

Notes

CHAPTER 1

1. *Popol Vuh: The Mayan Book of the Dawn of Life*, trans. Dennis Tedlock (New York: Simon and Schuster, 1996).

2. John Bierhorst, *History and Mythology of the Aztecs: The Codex Chimalpopoca* (Tucson: University of Arizona Press, 1998), contains the complete text of the codex "Legend of the Suns," which was based on earlier oral and inscribed sources on the origin of the Aztecs.

3. Richard E. W. Adams, "Introduction to a Survey of the Native Prehistoric Cultures of Mesoamerica," in *The Cambridge History of the Native Peoples of the Americas*, vol. 2, *Mesoamerica*, ed. Richard E. W. Adams and Murdo J. MacLeod (New York: Cambridge University Press, 1998), 7–12.

4. Susan Kellogg, *Weaving the Past* (New York: Oxford University Press, 2005), 12–13.

5. Richard A. Diehl, *The Olmecs: America's First Civilization* (London: Thames and Hudson, 2004).

6. Michael Coe, *The Maya*, 7th ed., (New York: Thames and Hudson, 2005).

7. René Millon, "Teotihuacan: City, State, and Civilization," in *Supplement to the Handbook of Middle American Indians*, vol. 1, *Archaeology*, ed. Jeremy A. Sabloff (Austin: University of Texas Press, 1981), 208.

8. Michael C. Meyer and Susan M. Deeds, *The Course of Mexican History*, 9th ed. (New York: Oxford University Press, 2010), 31.

9. H. B. Nicholson, *Topiltzin Quetzalcoatl: The Once and Future Lord of the Toltecs* (Boulder: University Press of Colorado, 2001).

10. Eric Wolf, *Sons of the Shaking Earth: The People of Mexico and Guatemala— Their Land, History, and Culture* (Chicago: University of Chicago Press, 1959), 122.

11. Bruce E. Byland and John M. D. Pohol, *In The Realm of Eight Deer: The Archaeology of the Mixtec Codices* (Norman: University of Oklahoma Press, 1994); Philip Dark, *Mixtec Ethnohistory: A Method of Analysis of the Codical Art* (Oxford: Oxford University Press, 1959).

12. The Codex Azcatitlan was painted sometime in the sixteenth or seventeenth century and contains a gloss; it is currently located in the Bibliothèque Nationale in Paris. A succinct description, with images is found in Angela Marie Herren, "Portraying the Aztec Past in the Codex Azcatitlan: Colonial Strategies," *Athanor* 22 (2004), 6–13.

13. Ross Hassig, *War and Society in Ancient Mesoamerica* (Berkeley: University of California Press, 1992).

14. Bierhorst, *History and Mythology of the Aztecs*, 7.

15. This description comes from 1840, written by the Scottish American wife of the Spanish minister to Mexico. She noted that this kind of farming on the floating gardens had been practiced by the Aztecs using the same methods. Frances Calderón de la Barca, *Life in Mexico* (Garden City, N.Y.: Doubleday, 1965), 128.

16. Elizabeth Hill Boone, *The Aztec World* (New York: HarperCollins, 1995).

17. John Curl, *Inca, Maya and Aztec Poetry: Translations and Biographies of the Poets* (Tempe: Arizona State University Press, 2006), 45.

18. Codex Florentino in *The Broken Spears: The Aztec Account of the Conquest of Mexico,* ed. Miguel Leon-Portilla and trans. Lysander Kemp (Boston: Beacon Press, 1962), 6.

19. Michael E. Smith, *The Aztecs*, 2nd ed. (Malden, Mass.: Blackwell, 2003).

CHAPTER 2

1. Bernal Díaz, *The Conquest of New Spain*, trans. J. M. Cohen (Harmondsworth, UK: Penguin, 1963), 217.

2. There are numerous copies of Cortés's *Letters*. This translation of Second Letter to the King comes from Hernán Cortés, *Letters from Mexico*, trans. Anthony Pagden (New Haven, Conn.: Yale University Press, 1986), 160–82.

3. Díaz, *Conquest of New Spain,* 284–307.

4. Miguel Leon-Portilla, ed., *The Broken Spears: The Aztec Account of the Conquest of Mexico*, trans. from Nahuatl by Angel Maria Gariby and from Spanish by Lysander Kemp (Boston: Beacon Press, 1962), 138.

5. Ibid., 137–38.

6. Matthew Restall, *Seven Myths of the Spanish Conquest* (New York: Oxford University Press, 2003), 1–27; Laura E. Matthew and Michel R. Oudijk, eds., *Indian Conquistadors: Indigenous Allies in the Conquest of Mesoamerica* (Norman: University of Oklahoma Press, 2007), 44–54.

7. Cortés, *Letters*, 183–94.

8. Robert Ricard, *The Spiritual Conquest of Mexico* (Berkeley: University of California Press, 1966).

9. Susan M. Deeds, *Defiance and Deference in Mexico's Colonial North: Indians under Spanish Rule in Nueva Vizcaya* (Austin: University of Texas Press, 2003).

10. Bartolome de las Casas, *A Brief Account of the Destruction of the Indies*, trans. Nigel Griffin (New York: Penguin Books, 1992), 5. First published in 1542.

11. Charles Gibson, *The Aztecs under Spanish Rule: A History of the Indians of the Valley of Mexico, 1519–1810* (Stanford: Stanford University Press, 1964), 148–76.

12. Linda Curcio-Nagy, *The Great Festivals of Colonial Mexico City: Performing Power and Identity* (Albuquerque: University of New Mexico Press, 2004), 85–97.

13. Stafford Poole, *Our Lady of Guadalupe: The Origins and Sources of a Mexican National Symbol, 1531–1797* (Tucson: University of Arizona Press, 1995), 26–34.

14. Octavio Paz, *Sor Juana. Or, The Traps of Faith*, trans. Margaret Sayers Peden (Cambridge, Mass.: Harvard University Press, 1988).

15. Stephanie Merrim, *Feminist Perspectives on Sor Juana Inés de la Cruz* (Detroit: Wayne State University Press, 1999). There is also a film about her life, *Yo, la peor de todas* (*I, the Worst of All*), written and directed in 1990 by María Luisa Bemberg. Her complete writings and discussion of her intellectual world is available through the Sor Juana Inés de la Cruz Project, sponsored by The Department of Spanish and Portuguese, Dartmouth College, Hanover, New Hampshire.

16. Susan M. Deeds, "The Enlightened Colony," in *Companion to Mexican History and Culture*, ed. Williams H. Beezley (Malden, Mass.: Wiley-Blackwell, 2011).

CHAPTER 3

1. Michael C. Meyer, William L. Sherman, and Susan M. Deeds, *The Course of Mexican History* (New York: Oxford University Press, 2010), 222. For a full discussion of the reconstruction of the Grito de Dolores, see Isabel Fernández Tejedo and Carmen Nava, "Images of Independence in the Nineteenth Century: The Grito de Dolores, History and Myth," in *¡Viva México! ¡La Independencia! Celebrations of September 16*, ed. William H. Beezley and David Lorey (Wilmington, Del.: SR Books, 2000), 1–42.

2. Fernández Tejedo and Nava, "Images of Independence," 11.

3. Joel Roberts Poinsett, *Notes on Mexico made in the Autumn, 1822* (New York: Praeger, 1969), 68.

4. Christon I. Archer, "Fashioning a New Nation," in *The Oxford History of Mexico*, 2nd ed., ed. William H. Beezley and Michael C. Meyer (New York: Oxford University Press, 2010), 285–318.

5. David M. Pletcher, *The Diplomacy of Annexation: Texas, Oregon, and the Mexican War* (Columbia: University of Missouri Press, 1973).

6. Will Fowler, *Santa Anna of Mexico* (Lincoln: University of Nebraska Press, 2009), 43–70.

7. Christon I. Archer, "Independence and the Generation of Generals, 1810–1848," in *The Companion to Mexican History and Culture*, ed. William H. Beezley (Malden, Mass.: Wiley-Blackwell, 2011).

CHAPTER 4

1. John S. D. Eisenhower, *So Far from God: The U.S. War with Mexico, 1846–1848* (New York: Random House, 1989); Bernard DeVoto, *The Year of Decision 1846* (Boston: Houghton Mifflin, 1943).

2. Milo Milton Quaife, ed., *The Diary of James K. Polk during his Presidency, 1845–1849* (Chicago: A. C. McClury, 1910), 1:384–87.

3. This quotation comes from the Avalon Project: Documents in Law, History, and Diplomacy, Yale University Law School, http://avalon.law.yale.edu/19th_century/guadhida.asp#art7. Also see Teaching with Documents: The Treaty of Guadalupe Hidalgo, essay by Tom Gray, National Archives: Educators and Students, http://www.archives.gov/education/lessons/guadalupe-hidalgo/#documents.

4. Richard Griswold del Castillo, *The Treaty of Guadalupe Hidalgo: A Legacy of Conflict* (Norman: University of Oklahoma Press, 1990), 43–87.

5. Mark Pedelty, *Musical Ritual in Mexico City* (Austin: University of Texas Press, 2004), 9; Jesus C. Romero, *Verdadera historia del himno nacional mexicano* (Mexico City: Talleres Gráficas de la Nación, 1987); and the website on the national anthem, http://www.inside-mexico.com/anthem.htm.

6. Ralph Roeder, *Juárez and His Mexico* (New York: Viking Press, 1947), 1:122–35.

7. Jürgen Buchenau, "Small Numbers, Great Impact: Mexico and Its Immigrants, 1821–1973," *Journal of American Ethnic History* 20, no. 3 (2001): 23–49.

8. Brian Hammett, *Juárez* (London: Longman, 1994), 43–72.

9. Griselda Álvarez, "Manifiesto a la epístola de Melchor Ocampo (derechos y deberes de la mujer dentro del matrimonio civil)," *Fem Magazine* January 1, 2004.

10. Egon Corti, *Maxmilian and Charlotte of Mexico*, 2 vols. (New York: Knopf, 1928).

11. Paul Garner, *Porfirio Díaz* (London: Longman, 2001), 1–67.

CHAPTER 5

1. Paul Garner, *Porfirio Díaz* (London: Longman, 2001.

2. Don Coerver, *The Porfirian Interregnum: The Presidency of Manuel González of Mexico, 1880–1884* (Ft. Worth: Texas Christian University Press, 1979).

3. Stephen Neufeld, "Servants of the Nation: The Military in the Making of Modern Mexico, 1876–1911" (Ph.D. diss., University of Arizona, 2009).

4. Paul Vanderwood, *Disorder and Progress: Bandits, Police and Mexican Development*, rev. ed. (Wilmington, Del.: SR Books, 1992), 101–51.

5. Mauricio Tenorio Trillo, *Mexico at the World's Fairs: Crafting a Modern Nation* (Berkeley: University of California Press, 1996), 64–125.

6. William H. Beezley, *Judas at the Jockey Club*, 2nd ed. (Lincoln: University of Nebraska Press, 2004).

7. The information for each family comes from *Diccionario Porrúa de historia, biografía y geografía de México* (Mexico City: Editorial Porrúa, 1995) under the entries for the family name.

8. José Vasconcelos, *Don Evaristo Madero* (Mexico City: Impresiones Modernas, 1958).

9. The army and navy establishment served the far-flung British Empire and other consumers. It required customers to deposit money into an account, then order out of its catalog.

10. See "The Creelman Interview," http://www.emersonkent.com/historic_documents/creelman_interview_1908_original.htm, and in *The Mexico Reader: History, Culture, and Politics*, ed. Gilbert M. Joseph and Thomas J. Henderson (Durham, N.C.: Duke University Press, 2003), 285–91.

11. Mauricio Tenorio Trillo, "1910 Mexico City: Space and Nation in the City of the Centenario," in *¡Viva Mexico! ¡Viva la Independencis! Celebrations of September 16*, ed. William H. Beezley and David E. Lorey (Wilmington, Del.: SR Books, 2001), 167–98.

CHAPTER 6

1. William H. Beezley and Colin M. MacLachlan, *Mexicans in Revolution, 1910–1946* (Lincoln: University of Nebraska Press, 2009).

2. Jocelyn Olcott, Mary Kay Vaughan, and Gabriela Cano, eds., *Sex in Revolution: Gender, Politics, and Power in Modern Mexico* (Durham, N.C.: Duke University Press, 2006), 1–35.

3. Robert McCaa, "Missing Millions: The Demographic Costs of the Mexican Revolution," *Mexican Studies/Estudios Mexicanos* 19 (2003): 367–400.

4. James W. Wilkie, *The Mexican Revolution: Federal Expenditure and Social Change since 1910* (Berkeley: University of California Press, 1967), 194.

5. Ibid., 102–3, 293.

6. Ibid., 160.

7. See Rick Lopez, "The India Bonita Contest of 1921 and the Ethnicization of Mexican National Culture," *Hispanic American Historical Review* 82 (2002): 291–328, especially 305.

8. Mauricio Tenorio-Trillo, "The Cosmopolitan Summer, 1920–1949," *Latin American Research Review* 32 (1997): 224–42.

9. Alan Knight, "Cardenismo: Juggernaut or Jalopy?" *Journal of Latin American Studies* 26 (1994): 73–107.

10. Ibid., 105–7.

11. Gene Gurney, *Pictorial History of the US Army* (New York: Random House, 1982), 45.

12. Wilkie, *Mexican Revolution*, 160.

CHAPTER 7

1. Paul Gillingham, "Sex, Death and Structuralism: Alternative Views of the 20th Century," in *A Companion to Mexican History and Culture*, ed. William H. Beezley (Malden, Mass.: Wiley-Blackwell, 2011).

2. Roderic Ai Camp, "Education and Political Recruitment in Mexico: The Alemán Generation," *Journal of Inter-American Studies and World Affairs* 8 (1976): 295–321.

3. Julio Moreno, *Yankee Don't Go Home! Mexican Nationalism, American Business Culture, and the Shaping of Modern Mexico, 1920–1950* (Chapel Hill: University of North Carolina Press, 2003), 112–52.

4. Roderic A. Camp, "The Revolution's Second Generation: The Miracle, 1946–1982 and Collapse of the PRI, 1982–2000," in *A Companion to Mexican History and Culture*, ed. William H. Beezley (Malden, Mass.: Wiley-Blackwell, 2011).

5. James W. Wilkie, *The Mexican Revolution: Federal Expenditure and Social Change since 1910* (Berkeley: University of California Press, 1970), chart on 167.

6. Kevin B. Witherspoon, *Before the Eyes of the World: Mexico and the 1968 Olympic Games* (DeKalb: Northern Illinois University Press, 2008), 74–93.

7. Ariel Rodríguez Kuri, "Challenges, Political Opposition, Economic Disaster, Natural Disaster, and Democratization, 1968 to 2000," *A Companion to Mexican History and Culture,* ed. William H. Beezley (Malden, Mass.: Wiley-Blackwell, 2011).

8. See both Elena Poniatowska, *Massacre in Mexico* (Columbia: University of Missouri Press, 1992), and http://socialistdemocracy.wordpress.com/2008/08/07/the-1968-mexican-student-rebellion/.

9. Rodríguez Kuri, "Challenges."

10. Amelia Kiddle and Maria Múñoz, eds., *Populism in Twentieth Century Mexico: Populism in Mexico under Lázaro Cárdenas and Luis Echeverría* (Tucson: University of Arizona Press, 2010), especially William H. Beezley, "Gabardine Suits and Guayabera Shirts: Some Comments on the Populist Political styles of Lázaro Cárdenas and Luis Echeverría," 190–206.

11. Rodríguez Krui, "Challenges".

12. Kate Doyle "The Dawn of Mexico's Dirty War: Lucio Cabañas and the Party of the Poor," National Security Archive, http://www.gwu.edu/~nsarchiv/NSAEBB/NSAEBB105/index.htm.

13. Armando Bartra, "Piel de papel: Los pepines en la educación sentimental del mexicano," *Revista Latinoamericana de Estudios sobre la Historieta* 1 (2001): 67–90.

14. Roderic Ai Camp, *Mexico's Mandarins: Crafting a Power Elite for the Twenty-First Century* (Berkeley: University of California Press, 2002), 227.

15. Roderic A. Camp, "The Time of the Technocrats and Deconstruction of the Revolution," in *The Oxford History of Mexico*, 2nd ed., ed. Michael C. Meyer and William H. Beezley (New York: Oxford University Press, 2000), 609–36.

CHAPTER 8

1. Claudio Lomnitz, "Times of Crisis: Historicity, Sacrifice, and the Spectacle of Debacle in Mexico City," *Public Culture* 15 (2003): 127–47.

2. For a film about the police chief, see *Durazo: La Verdadera Historia* (1988), directed by Gilberto de Anda and starring Sergio Bustamante.

3. Elena Poniatowska, *Nothing, Nobody: The Voices of the Mexico City Earthquake*, trans. Arthur Schmidt and Aurora Comacho De Schmidt (Philadelphia: Temple University Press, 1995.

4. Roderic A. Camp, *The Metamorphosis of Leadership in a Democratic Mexico* (New York: Oxford University Press, 2010), 253–57.

5. Carrie C. Chorba, *Mexico, from Mestizo to Multicultural: National Identity and Recent Representations of the Conquest* (Nashville, Tenn.: Vanderbilt University Press, 2007), 2, 17–19.

6. "EZLN Communiques (1994–2004)," translated into English at http://www.struggle.ws/mexico/ezlnco.html.

7. Roderic Ai Camp, *Mexico's Mandarins: Crafting a Power Elite for the Twenty-First Century* (Berkeley: University of California Press, 2002), 234–41.

8. Joseph L Klesner, "The 2000 Mexican Presidential and Congressional Elections: Pre-Election Report," Western Hemisphere Election Study Series, XVIII, 1 (June 15, 2000), http://www.csis.org/americas/pubs/Klesner.pdf.

9. "Mexican Federal Elections 2000: Electoral Observation Report," report by Global Exchange and Alianza Cívica (Global Exchange, 2000), 7, http://www.globalexchange.org/countries/americas/mexico/election2000/ElectionReport.pdf.

10. Camp, *Metamorphosis of Leadership*, 387.

11. Ibid.

12. "Mexico Elections 2006," Mexico Institute, Woodrow Wilson International Center, http://www.wilsoncenter.org/index.cfm?topic_id=5949&fuseaction=topics.item&news_id=143858#archive.

13. Ibid.

14. *El Universal* (Mexico City), December 27, 2008.

15. "Drug Violence in Mexico: Data and Analysis from 2001–2009" (Trans-Border Institute, University of San Diego, 2010), available online from the Mexico Institute, Woodrow Wilson International Center, http://www.wilsoncenter.org/index.cfm?topic_id=5949&fuseaction=topics.item&news_id=143858#archive. This report provides references to governmental and journalistic investigations.

16. Philippa Strum and Andrew Selee, eds., "The Hispanic Challenge? What We Know about Latino Immigration" (Woodrow Wilson International Center for Scholars), available online from the Mexico Institute, Woodrow Wilson International Center, http://www.wilsoncenter.org/index.cfm?topic_id=5949&fuseaction=topics.item&news_id=143858#archive. This report provides references to governmental and journalistic investigations; Timothy J. Henderson, "Mexican Immigration to the United States," in *A Companion to Mexican History and Culture*, ed. William H. Beezley (Malden, Mass.: Wiley-Blackwell, 2010).

Further Reading

GENERAL HISTORIES

Beezley, William H. and Michael C.Meyer, eds. *The Oxford History of Mexico.*
2nd ed. New York: Oxford University Press, 2010.

Camp, Roderic Ai. *Mexico: What Everyone Needs to Know.* New York: Oxford
University Press, 2011.

Jaffary, Nora E., Edward W. Osowski, and Susie S. Porter, eds. *Mexican History:
A Primary Source Reader.* Philadelphia: Westview Press, 2010.

Meyer, Michael C., and Susan Deeds. *The Course of Mexican History.* 8th ed. New
York: Oxford University Press, 2010.

Tuñón, Julia. *Women in Mexico: A Past Unveiled.* Austin: University of Texas Press,
1999.

INDIGENOUS MEXICO

Adams, Richard E. W., and Murdo J. MacLeon, eds. *The Cambridge History of the
Native Peoples of the Americas.* Vol. 2, *Mesoamerica.* New York: Cambridge
University Press, 1998.

Boone, Elizabeth Hill. *Red and Black: Pictorial Histories of the Aztecs and Mixtec.*
Austin: University of Texas Press, 2000.

Codex Florentine. Facsimile reproduction. 4 vols. Mexico: Libros Mas Cultura, 2010.

Coe, Michael, and Richard A. Diehl. *In the Land of the Olmec.* 2 vols. Austin:
University of Texas Press, 1980.

León-Portilla, Miguel. *The Aztec Image of Self and Society: An Introduction to Nahua
Culture.* Edited by José Klor de Alva. Salt Lake City: University of Utah Press and
School of American Research, 1952.

Schele, Linda, and David Friedel. *A Forest of Kings: The Untold Story of the Ancient
Maya.* New York: Morrow, 1990.

Schroeder, Susan. *Chimalpahin and the Kingdom of Chalco.* Tucson: University of
Arizona Press, 1991.

Wolf, Eric. *Sons of the Shaking Earth: The People of Mexico and Guatemala—Their
Land, History, and Culture.* Chicago: University of Chicago Press, 1974.

COLONIAL NEW SPAIN

Bennett, Herman L. *Africans in Colonial Mexico: Absolutism, Christianity and
Afro-Creole Consciousness, 1570–1640.* Bloomington: Indiana University Press,
2003.

Cortés, Hernán. *Hernán Cortés: Letters from Mexico.* New York: Orion Press, 1971.

Crosby, Alfred W. *The Columbian Exchange: Ecological and Cultural Consequences of
1492.* Westport, Conn.: Greenwood Press, 1972.

Curcio Nagy, Linda. *The Great Festivals of Colonial Mexico City: Performing Power
and Identity.* Albuquerque: University of New Mexico Press, 2004.

Deeds, Susan M. *Defiance and Deference in Colonial Mexico: Indians under Spanish Rule in Nueva Vizcaya*. Austin: University of Texas Press, 2003.

Díaz del Castillo, Bernal. *The True History of the Conquest of New Spain, 1517–1521*. New York: Farrar, Straus and Giroux, 1966.

Gibson, Charles. *The Aztecs under Spanish Rule: A History of the Indians of the Valley of Mexico, 1519–1810*. Stanford, Calif.: Stanford University Press, 1964.

Leonard, Irving. *Baroque Times in Old Mexico: Seventeenth-Century Persons, Places and Practices*. Ann Arbor: University of Michigan Press, 1971.

León-Portilla, Miguel, ed. *The Broken Spears. The Aztec Account of the Conquest of Mexico*. Boston: Beacon Press, 1972.

Melville, Elinor G. K. *A Plague of Sheep: Environmental Consequences of the Conquest of Mexico*. Cambridge: Cambridge University Press, 1994.

Mills, Kenneth, and William B. Taylor, eds. *Colonial Spanish America: A Documentary History*. Wilmington, Del.: SR Books, 1998.

Restall, Matthew. *Seven Myths of the Spanish Conquest*. New York: Oxford University Press, 2003.

Schurz, William L. *The Manila Galleon*. New York: Dutton, 1939.

Taylor, William B. *Landlord and Peasant in Colonial Oaxaca*. Stanford, Calif.: Stanford University Press, 1972.

Weber, David J. *The Spanish Frontier in North America*. New Haven, Conn.: Yale University Press, 1992.

NINETEENTH-CENTURY MEXICO

Beezley, William H. *Judas at the Jockey Club and Other Episodes of Porfirian Mexico*. 2nd ed. Lincoln: University of Nebraska Press, 2004.

———. *Mexican National Identity: Memory, Innuendo, and Popular Culture*. Tucson: University of Arizona Press, 2008.

Brading, David A. *The First America: The Spanish Monarchy, Creole Patriots and the Liberal State, 1492–1866*. Cambridge: Cambridge University Press, 1993.

Calderón de la Barca, Fanny. *Life in Mexico: The Letters of Fanny Calderón de la Barca*. Edited by Howard T. Fisher and Marion Hall Fisher. Garden City, N.Y.: Doubleday, 1970.

Garner, Paul. *Porfirio Díaz*. London: Longman, 2001.

Guardino, Peter F. *Peasants, Politics, and the Formation of Mexico's National State: Guerrero, 1800–1867*. Stanford, Calif.: Stanford University Press, 1996.

Hale, Charles A. *Mexican Liberalism in the Age of Mora, 1821–1853*. New Haven, Conn.: Yale University Press, 1968.

———. *The Transformation of Liberalism in Late Nineteenth-Century Mexico*. Princeton, N.J.: Princeton University Press, 1989.

Hamnett, Brian. *Juárez*. London: Longman, 1994.

Hart, John M. *Empire and Revolution: The Americas in Mexico since the Civil War*. Berkeley: University of California Press, 2002.

Henderson, Timothy J. *A Glorious Defeat: Mexico and Its War with the United States*. New York: Farrar, Straus and Giroux, 2008.

Joseph, Gilbert M., and Timothy J. Henderson, eds. *The Mexico Reader: History, Culture, Politics*. Durham, N.C.: Duke University Press, 2003.

Rugeley, Terry. *Of Wonders and Wise Men: Religion and Popular Cultures in Southeastern Mexico, 1800–1876*. Austin: University of Texas Press, 2001.

Weber, David J. *The Mexican Frontier, 1821–1846: The American Southwest under Mexico*. Albuquerque: University of New Mexico Press, 1982.

TWENTIETH-CENTURY MEXICO

Anderson, Joan B., and James Gerber. *Fifty Years of Change on the U.S.-Mexico Border: Growth, Development, and Quality of Life*. Austin: University of Texas Press, 2007.

Bailey, David C. *¡Viva Cristo Rey! The Cristero Rebellion and the Church-State Conflict in Mexico*. Austin: University of Texas Press, 1974.

Camp, Roderic Ai. *Mexico's Mandarins: Crafting a Power Elite for the Twenty-First Century*. Berkeley: University of California Press, 2002.

———. *Politics in Mexico: The Democratic Consolidation*. New York: Oxford University Press, 2006.

Dulles, John W. F. *Yesterday in Mexico: A Chronicle of the Revolution, 1919–1930*. Austin: University of Texas Press, 1961.

Harris, Charles H., and Louis R. Sadler. *The Secret War in El Paso: Mexican Revolutionary Intrigue, 1906–1920*. Albuquerque: University of New Mexico Press, 2009.

Joseph, Gilbert M., Anne Rubenstein, and Eric Zolov, eds. *Fragments of the Golden Age: The Politics of Culture in Mexico since 1940*. Durham, N.C.: Duke University Press, 2001.

Katz, Friedrich. *The Life and Times of Pancho Villa*. Stanford, Calif.: Stanford University Press, 1998.

Knight, Alan. *The Mexican Revolution*. 2 vols. New York: Cambridge University Press, 1986.

Poniatowska, Elena. *Massacre in Mexico*. New York: Viking, 1975.

Rosalie Evans Letters from Mexico. Arranged with comments by Daisy Caden Pettus. Indianapolis, Ind.: Bobbs-Merrill, 1926.

Vaughan, Mary Kay. *Cultural Politics in Revolution: Teachers, Peasants and Schools in Mexico, 1930–1940*. Tucson: University of Arizona Press, 1996.

Vaughan, Mary Kay, and Steven E. Lewis, eds. *The Eagle and the Virgin: Nation and Cultural Revolution in Mexico, 1920–1940*. Durham, N.C.: Duke University Press, 2006.

Wilkie, James W. *The Mexican Revolution: Federal Expenditure and Social Change since 1910*. Berkeley: University of California Press, 1967.

Womack, John. *Zapata and the Mexican Revolution*. New York: Knopf, 1968.

Websites

Ancient Scripts
www.ancientscripts.com/aztec.html
> An introduction to the Aztec language, Nahuatl, with detailed explanations and illustrations of the writing system.

The Archive of Early American Images
www.brown.edu/Facilities/John_Carter_Brown_Library/pages/ea_hmpg.html
> A searchable archive of images of the Americas, 1492 to 1825, from the John Carter Brown Library at Brown University.

BBC News: Mexico Country Profile
http://news.bbc.co.uk/2/hi/americas/country_profiles/1205074.stm
> Overview of politics and economy; links to major Mexican newspapers, radio, and television shows; basic list of facts; time line; audio clip of the national anthem; and list of related BBC news stories.

Dumbarton Oaks Museum
www.doaks.org/museum
> This museum, run by Harvard University, contains a premier collection of Pre-Columbian art: Browse by the name of collections, culture, or medium, zoom to view details, and read detailed descriptions of each piece.

Latin American Network Information Center: Mexico
http://lanic.utexas.edu/la/mexico
> This list of links covers many topics, including anthropology and archaeology, arts and humanities, economy, government, history, and indigenous peoples.

Library of Congress Country Study: Mexico
http://memory.loc.gov/frd/cs/profiles/Mexico.pdf
> A lengthy overview of Mexican history and current events, written by the Federal Research Division.

The Life and Times of Frida Kahlo
www.pbs.org/weta/fridakahlo
> A companion website to the documentary film, with paintings by the artist, articles on her, the context of her life, and links to related sites.

Mesolore: A Cybercenter for Research and Teaching on Mesoamerica
www.mesolore.net
> Interactive primary sources and teaching tools on Mesoamerica. Developed at Brown University, the site includes an atlas, several codices with transcripts, videos, lectures, a glossary, and an index.

Mexconnect
www.mexconnect.com
> An electronic magazine about Mexican culture, travel, and business.

The Mexico Institute
www.wilsoncenter.org/index.cfm?fuseaction=topics.home&topic_id=5949
> The Mexico Institute at the Woodrow Wilson International Center posts news, event announcements, scholarly articles, and blog entries on the following topics: Migration and Migrants, Security and the Rule of Law, Economic Integration, Media and Society, Energy and Natural Resources, U.S.-Mexico Border, Politics, and Elections.

A Nation Emerges: Sixty-Five Years of Photography in Mexico
www.getty.edu/research/tools/guides_bibliographies/photography_mexico
> Browse or search albumen, collodion, and gelatin silver prints, cartes-de-visite, cabinet cards, photo albums, and postcards of Mexico from the Getty Research Institute, covering 1857 through the 1920s.

Native American Images
www.amphilsoc.org/library/digcoll/
natam
> Digitized items from the American
> Philosophical Society's collection that
> contain images of Native Americans.
> Includes manuscript materials on the
> Aztecs.

**Southwestern and Mexican Photography
Collection**
www.thewittliffcollections.txstate.edu/
collections/southwestern-mexican-
photography.html
> A collection of more than 150
> photographers' work, held at the
> Witliff Collections, Texas State
> University, San Marcos.

The Spanish American Revolutions
www.brown.edu/Facilities/John_Carter_
Brown_Library/spanishstage/index.html
> The John Carter Brown Library at
> Brown University created this online
> exhibit in celebration of the
> bicentennial of the independence of
> Spanish America. It covers the topics
> of the Age of Enlightenment, the
> Bourbon Reforms, and the Age of
> Atlantic Revolutions, Creole

Patriotism and the Public Sphere in
Spanish American, Public Unrest, and
the Crisis of 1808.

**Spanish Historical Writing about the
New World**
www.brown.edu/Facilities/John_Carter_
Brown_Library/spanishhistorical/index.
html
> This online exhibit from the John
> Carter Brown Library includes short
> descriptions and images of the
> frontispieces of Spaniards' influential
> published tracts about the New
> World.

Timeline of Art History
www.metmuseum.org/toah
> Search the time line from the
> Metropolitan Museum of Art for
> Central America. This site
> contextualizes art within history and
> provides images and descriptions of
> the highlights in the museum's
> collection.

Trans-Border Institute
www.sandiego.edu/tbi
> This University of San Diego website
> provides information on crime, drugs,
> and politics in the border region.

Acknowledgments

I am grateful for the assistance I received in completing this book from the participants in all the Oaxaca Summer Institutes, in particular my colleagues Bill French, Guillermo Palacios, Ricardo Pérez Montfort, Monica Rankin, Ann Blum, Claudia Agostoni, Elisa Speckman, and Gabriela Soto Laveaga. As with all things Mexican, Carmen Nava proved invaluable. Moreover, I had the encouragement and help of my editor at Oxford University Press, Nancy Toff, and her assistant, Sonia Tycko. This book is dedicated to the future: Mathew, Virginia, Max Madrid, and Nicolas Beezley, and *como siempre para Blue*.

Index

Liberals. *See also* Díaz, Porfírío;
González, Manuel; Juárez,
Benito
  achievements following French
    intervention, 79–80
  borrowing of, 68
  constitution of 1857 and, 66–67
  economics and, 66
  immigration and, 66
  national anthem and, 62
  parallel government of, 67–68
  PLM, 98–99
  Revolution of Ayutla and, 65
  southern U.S. and, 64
  technology and transportation and,
    63–64
  United States-Mexican War
    aftermath and, 60–61
  vestigial colonial institutions and, 63
Lincoln, Abraham, 57
López Mateos, Adolfo, 127, 129
López Obrador, Andrés, 148–49
López Portillo, José, 135–37
Luis Orozco, Wistano, 98

Madero, Evaristo, 97
Madero, Francisco, 101–2, 104, 105,
    107
Madrazo, Carlos, 139
Madrazo, Roberto, 148–49
Madrid, Miguel de la, 136–38
Malinche, 19
Manila galleon, 36
Marcha, Pío, 46
March of Humanity (mural), 133
Marcos, Subcomandante, 143, 148
María Mata, José, 60–61, 64
massacre, Tlatelolco, 131–32
Massacre of Topilejo, 114
mathematics, Maya, 8
Maximilian (emperor), 70, 72–73,
    74–75, 76
Maya
  agriculture of, 7

calendar, 8
Classic Era, 7–9
creation myth, 1
disappearance of centers, 10
dress and appearance of, 8–9
locations of, 7, 8
mathematics, 8
Post-Classic Era, 12
religion, 9
trade, 7–8
Mejía, Tomás, 74, 75, 76
mestizos (mixed ethnicity), 34–35
Mexica. *See* Aztecs
Mexican Liberal Party (PLM), 98–99
Mexico, xiif, xiiif. *See also specific
    subject*
  biological diversity of, 3
  culture and, xvi
  global influence of, xi–xiv
  instability explanations, 55
Mexico City, 35, *150*, *151*
middling Mexicans
  construction projects and, 124–25
  entrepreneurs and, 125–26
  motto of, 120
  property ownership and, 124
  satires and, 125
  Sears corporation and, 123–24
migration, 2, 25–26, 150–51
mining, constitution of 1857 and,
    84–85
Miramón, Miguel, 68, 74, 75, 76
missionaries, 24–25, *25*, 33–34
Mixcoaltl, 11
Mixtecs, 12–13
*Modernization Proposals for the
    Agricultural and Livestock
    Industry* (Salinas de Gotarí), 141
Molina Enriquez, Andrés, 101
Monroe, James, 47
Monte Alban, 9, 10, 12–13
Montezuma II, 20–21
Mora y del Río, José, 112
Morelos, José María, 35, 43, 44–45